THE STEADY PRACTITIONER:

A GUIDE FOR THOSE WHO GUIDE OTHERS

By

Aethodios Brown

Table of Contents

Before We Begin

If you're reading this, chances are you've always been the one people come to.

Maybe it started in high school, when friends would pull you aside after class to ask what they should do about a crush or a fight with their parents. Maybe it was later, at work, when colleagues noticed you had a way of sensing the unspoken tension in a room. Or maybe it just happened naturally—the quiet friend, the good listener, the one whose words seem to land exactly where they need to.

At some point, someone probably said it: "You should do this for real. You should charge for this."

And maybe a part of you lit up at the thought, while another part felt a flutter of something else—doubt, maybe, or the quiet weight of wondering: Can I really hold that space for someone? What if I say the wrong thing? What if they lean on me and I'm not strong enough to hold them up?

That flutter is exactly why you need this book.

Not because you aren't capable. You clearly are. But because being capable and being a trusted guide are two very different things. One is a gift you were born with. The other is a role you grow into, carefully, deliberately, with eyes wide open to the responsibility it carries.

This book won't teach you how to be more intuitive. It won't give you secret techniques or mystical formulas. What it will do is help you build a container strong enough to hold the weight of what you already carry—for yourself, and for the people who will come to you when their own ground feels shaky.

We're going to walk through this together, one step at a time. And by the end, I hope you'll feel not just ready, but steady.

Chapter 1:

The Weight of Being Seen

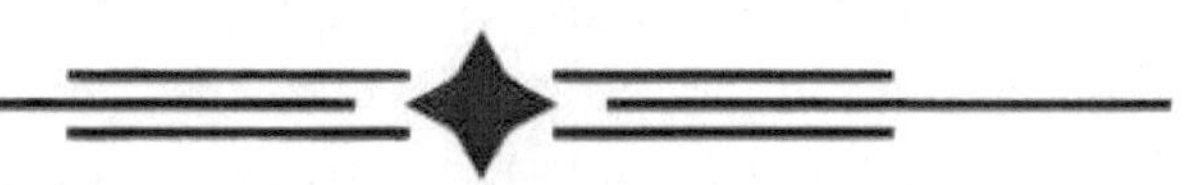

It always happens in an ordinary moment.

You're sitting across from someone, maybe in person or on a screen, and you say something that isn't particularly profound. Just an observation, really. Something you noticed in their voice or their posture or the way they keep circling back to the same point. It could also be something that you are hearing from their loved one on the other side, their spirit guide, from their Higher Power or the tarot cards. Maybe it was from their Higher Self, the divination tool or a member of their spirit team.

And then you see it.

Their shoulders drop. The tightness around their mouth softens. They exhale, long and slow, like they've been holding their breath for days. When they speak again, their voice is different—quieter, yes, but also more solid, as if they've just found something they didn't know they lost.

"Finally," they might say. "That makes sense."

In that moment, something has shifted. Not just in them, but in the space between you. You've crossed an invisible line without even realizing it. You're no longer just someone having a conversation. You're someone who made sense of the world for another person. And that changes everything.

The First Time It Really Hits You

I remember talking to a woman named Elena (not her real name) about her grandmother. She came to me because she was planning to quit her job, sell her apartment, move back to her hometown to care for this woman who raised her. She'd been wrestling with the decision for months, running the numbers, making pro and con lists, asking everyone she knew for advice.

Halfway through our conversation, I said something simple: "It sounds like you've already decided. You're just waiting for permission."

She stared at me for what felt like a full minute. Then she started to cry—not sad tears, but the kind that come when something inside you finally relaxes. "No one has ever said that to me," she whispered. "Everyone keeps giving me more things to think about. You're the first person who actually heard me."

In that moment, I understood something I hadn't fully grasped before: Elena didn't need more information. She needed someone to reflect back what she already knew but couldn't yet trust. She needed confirmation that her own inner voice was worth listening to.

That's what we do, isn't it? We give people permission to trust themselves.

The Hidden Weight of Your Words

Here's the thing about that moment of relief: it feels beautiful, and it is. But it also comes with a weight that's easy to miss when you're just starting out.

When someone relaxes into what you've said, they aren't just hearing you anymore. They're organizing themselves around your words. Your casual observation becomes their guiding principle. Your gentle suggestion becomes their new north star.

Most of the time, this is fine. You're careful, you're thoughtful, you mean well. But the weight doesn't come from your intention. It comes from their reception.

Consider these two very different ways of saying almost the same thing:

- "From what I'm hearing, it seems like communication might open up again if you both shift some patterns."
- "Don't worry. They'll be back in three months."

To you, as the guide, these might feel like stylistic differences—one more cautious, one more direct. But to the person on the other side, they land in completely different universes.

The first one invites participation. It says, "Here's a possibility. What do you think?" The second one replaces participation with waiting. It says, "Sit tight. Your life is on a schedule I can see and you can't."

Once waiting begins, something shifts. The client stops being an active participant in their own life and becomes a spectator. They delay decisions, stay in situations longer than they should, avoid hard conversations—not because they lack courage, but because they believe they've been told how the story ends.

And here's the really tricky part: you never said you were writing their story. You just made a comment. But to someone who came to you desperate for solid ground, that comment sounded like prophecy.

When Gratitude Becomes Something Else

It starts so innocently.

A client books another session "just to check in." Then they send a quick message a few days later "for clarity." Then another message, and another. Each time, they're polite, grateful, almost apologetic for reaching out. It feels like appreciation, like proof that you're helping.

But slowly, almost imperceptibly, the shape of the relationship changes. They stop making decisions without you. They hesitate before taking action, waiting to see if you'll weigh in. They begin to treat your availability as a kind of safety net, something to catch them whenever uncertainty strikes.

You didn't ask for this. You didn't encourage it. You just kept showing up, kept being kind, kept answering messages because that's what caring people do.

And now here you are, holding something you never meant to hold: not a client, but a dependence.

The hardest lesson many guides learn is that the very thing that makes you good at this—your genuine desire to help—can also be the thing that accidentally keeps people small. Every time you answer a question they could have answered themselves, you teach them to come to you first. Every time you provide reassurance outside a session, you reinforce the idea that stability lives in you, not in them.

This isn't manipulation. It's not even a choice, really. It's just how human brains work. Relief gets attached to its source. And once that attachment forms, it takes conscious, consistent effort to redirect it back where it belongs: inside the person themselves.

What It Means to Really Guide

A woman named Margaret came to see me years ago, shortly after her husband died. She was hollowed out, barely functioning, showing up to sessions because she didn't know what else to do with her days. For months, I held space for her grief. I let her cry, let her rage, let her sit in silence when words wouldn't come. I answered her late-night emails when the loneliness was too much to bear alone.

It felt like the right thing to do. And maybe it was, in those early, raw months.

But at some point, I had to shift. I had to start saying things like, "What do you think you need right now?" instead of "Here's what might help." I had to start responding to her messages the next morning instead of immediately at midnight. I had to trust that she could hold more than she believed she could.

It was terrifying. I felt cruel, distant, like I was abandoning her in her darkest hour.

But then something remarkable happened. Margaret started making her own decisions. She joined a grief group. She planned a trip to visit her sister. She called me before a session to say, "I almost cancelled because I realized I didn't actually need to come this week. I just wanted to tell you I'm okay."

That was the moment I understood what my job really is. Not to be the stable one forever, but to help someone find their own stability. Not to answer every question, but to help someone trust their own answers.

The Question That Changes Everything

Here's something I ask myself after every difficult session: Was I useful, or did I make myself necessary?

Useful means they walk away stronger. Necessary means they can't walk without me.

Useful means my words become tools they can use on their own. Necessary means my words become crutches they lean on.

Useful means I'm building something in them. Necessary means I'm building something between us.

The difference is subtle in the moment but enormous over time. And choosing useful over necessary, again and again, is what separates a guide who merely helps from one who truly heals.

Reflections for Your Own Journey

- Think about a time when someone really leaned on your words. What happened after that conversation? Did they grow stronger, or did they come back looking for more?
- When a client thanks you, what do you think they're really thanking you for—the information you gave, the relief they felt, or the certainty you provided?
- Is there a part of you that likes being needed? Be honest. What would it feel like to let that go?
- What would shift in your sessions if your main goal became helping someone trust their own decisions instead of resolving their uncertainty for them?

Chapter 2:

The Gift You Were Given Isn't the Practice You'll Build

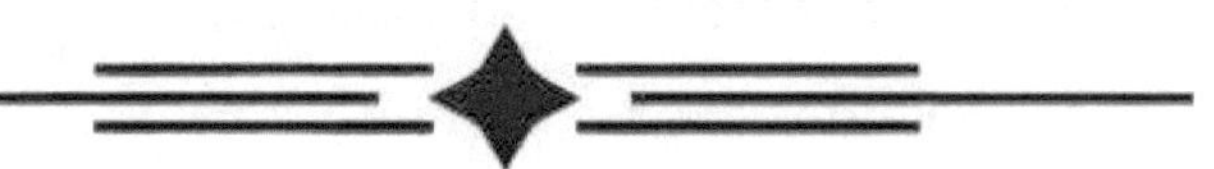

Everyone starts the same way.

Someone notices something about you. Maybe you have a knack for saying exactly what someone needs to hear. Maybe you sense things before they happen, or you pick up on dynamics that other people miss. Friends start seeking you out when they're confused or hurting. Strangers at parties end up telling you their life stories.

It feels like a gift, because it is. It came to you naturally, without effort, like a voice you've always been able to hear or a sight other people don't have.

And then one day, someone offers you money for it.

That moment changes everything. Not because money itself is transformative, but because payment introduces something that wasn't there before: expectation. Before money, you were helping because you cared. After money, you're providing a service. And services come with unspoken contracts, invisible rules about what's fair and what's not, what's included and what costs extra.

Most guides never think about this transition. They just accept the money and keep doing what they've always done. And then they wonder why things start to feel different—heavier, more draining, more complicated than before.

The Three Stages Nobody Tells You About

Whether you realize it or not, every guide moves through three distinct stages. Understanding them won't make the journey easier, exactly, but it will make it make sense.

Stage One: The Gifted Friend

This is where you start. You help because you care. There's no schedule, no set price, no boundary between your role and your personality. Your insight is just an extension of who you are, something you offer freely because it feels as natural as breathing.

People love you at this stage. They also take the most from you at this stage, because there are no visible edges to what you give. You're available at midnight, during your own hard days, when you're exhausted and empty and have nothing left to offer. You give anyway, because that's what friends do.

This stage can last for years. It feels authentic, untainted by the cold hand of commerce. But it's also unsustainable. You can't pour from an empty cup forever, and you can't set boundaries with people who don't know boundaries exist.

Stage Two: The Paid Helper

Eventually, someone insists on paying you. You hesitate, then accept. Money enters the exchange, but nothing else changes. You still don't have policies, limits, or clear expectations. You're just getting paid now.

This is where the trouble starts.

Clients message at all hours. They ask for refunds when they don't hear what they wanted. They book session after session without integrating anything between them. They lean on you harder than they leaned on you when you were free, because payment creates a sense of entitlement, an assumption that they've purchased access to you.

You're being treated like a professional without having built a professional framework. And obligation without structure becomes pressure, then resentment, then burnout.

Many guides quit here. They decide they aren't cut out for this work, when really, they just never built a container strong enough to hold it.

Stage Three: The Practice

A real practice begins when your service stops being an extension of your personality and becomes something separate from you. Something with predictable processes, clear boundaries, consistent language, and visible edges. Something that exists independently of your mood, your availability, your emotional state on any given day.

When you reach this stage, something surprising happens: you become both more respected and less drained. Clients know how to engage with you before they ever contact you. They show up prepared, with realistic expectations and respect for your time. They don't need you to explain the rules because the rules are visible from the start.

The practice holds the structure so you don't have to.

Why Talent Alone Will Wear You Down

A woman named Priya came to me years ago, exhausted and confused. She was the most intuitive person I'd ever met—her readings were uncannily accurate, the kind that make people gasp and cry and tell all their friends. She had a waiting list a mile long and more demand than she could possibly meet.

And she was miserable.

"I don't understand," she told me. "I'm good at this. I'm really good at this. So why do I dread every session? Why do I feel like I'm being drained instead of fulfilled?"

We started talking about her process, or rather, her lack of one. Priya had no boundaries. She gave clients her personal number. She answered messages at all hours. She let sessions run long because she couldn't bear to cut someone off mid-cry. She never said no, never set limits, never protected her own energy.

Her talent had created attention, but it hadn't created sustainability. The more accurate her insights, the more people wanted from her. And because she had no structure to contain those demands, they just kept coming, endless and overwhelming, until she had nothing left to give.

Talent without structure is like a fire without a fireplace. It gives light and warmth, sure, but eventually it spreads, consumes everything around it, and burns out because there's nothing left to fuel it. Whether its helping through structured sessions or workings that you are doing, no matter how good you are it can wear you and your loved ones out without the right structure and container.

The Myth of Keeping It Natural

There's a fear that runs through many guides: the worry that structure will make their work feel mechanical. That policies and boundaries will drain the magic out of what they do. That if they have to think about rules and limits, they'll lose the spontaneous connection that makes their insights powerful.

I understand that fear. I felt it too, once.

But here's what I've learned: structure doesn't remove care. Structure protects care from chaos.

Think about any profession that requires trust—medicine, counseling, law, teaching. The best doctors don't keep their patients waiting for hours because they don't care. They have schedules because schedules allow them to give each person focused attention. The best teachers don't answer emails at midnight because they're indifferent. They have boundaries because boundaries let them show up fresh and present for their students the next morning.

Structure doesn't make you cold. It makes you sustainable. And sustainability is the most caring thing you can offer, because it means you'll still be here next month, next year, next decade, ready to help the next person who needs you.

A Different Kind of Practice

I once worked with a guide named Samuel who ran his practice completely differently than anyone I'd met. He only saw three clients a day, never more. He had a strict 60-minute limit and ended sessions on the dot, no matter how emotional things got. He didn't give out his email or phone number. All communication went through a booking system that automatically scheduled follow-ups.

When I first heard about his approach, I thought it sounded rigid. Cold, even. How could anyone do deep work with so many constraints?

Then I sat in on one of his sessions.

The woman he was meeting with had just lost her son. She was raw, shattered, barely able to speak without weeping. And Samuel held her with such tenderness, such complete presence, that I forgot about the clock, forgot about the rules, forgot about everything except the sacred space they were creating together.

After exactly 60 minutes, he gently brought the session to a close. He reminded her of resources she could access between now and their next appointment. He thanked her for trusting him with her pain. And when she left, she looked steadier than when she arrived.

Later, Samuel told me something I've never forgotten: "The boundaries aren't for me. They're for her. She needs to know that this container is strong enough to hold her. She needs to trust that I'll be just as present next time as I was this time. She can't trust that if I'm exhausted and burned out and resentful. The boundaries protect her experience, not just my energy."

That's when I understood. Professionalism isn't the opposite of care. It's care organized into a form that can last.

What You're Really Building

When you build a practice, you're not building a business. Not really. You're building a container—a space where healing can happen safely, predictably, consistently. A space that exists whether you're having a good day or a bad one, whether you're energized or exhausted, whether you're feeling generous or protective of your time.

The container holds the work so the work doesn't spill everywhere.

It includes:

- Where sessions happen
- How long they last
- What topics are appropriate
- What happens between sessions
- What doesn't happen, ever

When your container is clear, something beautiful occurs: respectful clients feel comfortable, and difficult clients often self-select out before problems begin. Not because you're exclusionary, but because you're clear. And clarity attracts people who are ready for what you offer.

The Moment It Becomes Real

Your practice becomes real the day a stranger can engage with your service without knowing you personally.

If someone can visit your website, read your policies, understand what you do and how you do it, and book a session without ever having a conversation with you—that's the moment you've moved from gifted person to professional guide. That's the moment your practice exists independently of you, as a thing in the world that people can find and use and trust.

From this point forward, growth becomes possible without overwhelm. Each new client receives the same clarity as the last. Each session reinforces the structure instead of testing it. And most importantly, you're no longer required to be constantly available to be effective.

You've built something that works, whether you're working or not.

Reflections for Your Own Journey

- Which stage are you in right now—gifted friend, paid helper, or structured practice? Be honest with yourself.
- What expectations do your clients currently have that you never actually agreed to? List them.
- In one sentence, what do you actually provide? Try to write it without using words like "healing" or "transformation."
- What part of creating more structure feels uncomfortable? What are you afraid might happen?

Chapter 3:

The Quiet Difference Between Being Liked and Being Trusted

Early in my work, I confused them constantly.

I thought being liked meant I was doing something right. When clients thanked me profusely, when they told me I was the only one who understood them, when they came back again and again and again—I took it as proof that I was helping.

It took me years to understand that gratitude isn't the same as growth. And that being deeply liked can actually be a warning sign, a signal that I'm providing comfort instead of guidance, reassurance instead of real support.

The distinction changed everything.

Why Warmth Isn't Enough

There's a guide I know named Theresa who's beloved by her clients. They gush about her in online forums. They send her gifts on her birthday. They refer their friends with evangelical fervor. By every external measure, she's wildly successful.

But Theresa is not only tired but also exhausted. Her clients message her constantly, expecting responses within hours. They get hurt when she doesn't remember details from previous sessions. They book follow-ups before they've had time to integrate anything from the last one. They love her, yes, but their love feels more like need than appreciation.

Theresa built her practice on warmth. She's genuinely caring, genuinely present, genuinely invested in her clients' well-being. And that warmth attracted people who were hungry for exactly that—warmth, connection, the feeling of being truly seen and cared for.

But warmth without structure becomes a trap. It attracts people who are looking for someone to hold them, not someone to help them stand. And those people never leave, because leaving would mean losing the warmth they've come to depend on.

The Different Feeling of Trust

I think about a different guide, a man named Richard who's been practicing for over thirty years. Richard isn't warm in the way Theresa is. He's calm, steady, consistent—but not effusive. He doesn't gush. He doesn't over-share. He doesn't make clients feel like they're his new best friend.

And yet, his clients trust him implicitly. They don't message him between sessions because they know he won't respond. They don't get hurt when he ends on time because they know that's part of the container. They come to him for perspective, not reassurance, and they leave feeling stronger, not just soothed.

Richard's clients don't love him the way Theresa's clients love her. But they respect him in a way her clients don't respect her. And respect, I've learned, is what makes guidance stick.

The Moment I Learned the Difference

Years ago, I had a client named Angela who was stuck in a terrible relationship. She came to me week after week, crying about the same fights, the same disappointments, the same hopes that maybe this time would be different. And week after week, I listened. I validated. I offered comfort and perspective and gentle suggestions for change.

Nothing shifted.

One day, in frustration, I said something different. I said, "Angela, I've noticed something. Every week you come here and tell me about the same pain. And every week, I give you the same kind of support. And nothing changes. I wonder if the support I'm giving is actually helping you stay stuck."

She stared at me, hurt flickering across her face. For a terrible moment, I thought I'd ruined everything.

Then she took a shaky breath and said, "No one has ever said that to me before. Everyone just listens and feels sorry for me. I think I needed someone to stop feeling sorry for me."

That conversation was a turning point—for Angela, yes, but even more so for me. I realized that my warmth, my willingness to listen without challenging and trying to be so overly-accepting, had been part of the problem. I'd been so afraid of not being liked that I'd failed to be useful. My trained conditional self-worth and approval-based identity was a hindrance to both myself and Angela.

What People Actually Need

Here's something I've come to understand: people don't come to you because they want to feel good. They come because they want to feel better—and those aren't the same thing.

Feeling good is temporary relief. It's the warmth of being understood, the comfort of having someone nod along with your story. It matters, sure, but it doesn't change anything. You can feel good for an hour and then walk back into the exact same life, the exact same patterns, the exact same pain.

Feeling better is different. Feeling better means something inside you has shifted. You see your situation differently. You understand your role in it more clearly. You have new tools, new questions, new ways of approaching what's hard. You're not just soothed—you're strengthened.

Warmth gives people the first. Trust gives them the second.

The Quiet Work of Building Trust

Trust isn't built in dramatic moments. It's built in the ordinary ones—the sessions that end on time, the boundaries that stay consistent, the responses that remain steady even when clients push against them.

Trust is built when you say no calmly, without apology. When you hold the structure even when someone begs you to bend it. When you tell the truth about what you see, even if it's not what they want to hear. When you remain the same person session after session, predictable in your presence, reliable in your care.

It doesn't feel flashy. It doesn't generate testimonials about how amazing you are. But it generates something better: clients who come back because they know what to expect, who refer others because they trust you'll treat their friends the same way, who leave your sessions stronger than they arrived.

That's the work. Not being liked, but being relied upon. Not warming people up, but steadying them down.

Reflections for Your Own Journey

- Think about a professional you deeply trust—a doctor, a teacher, a mentor. What specific behaviors make them feel reliable?
- Have you ever softened what you said because you were afraid of disappointing a client? When?
- After your sessions, do clients usually ask follow-up questions right away, or do they come back later with new experiences to share?
- What's one way you could make your communication more consistent, starting this week?

Chapter 4:

The Slow Creep of Dependence

It never announces itself.

There's no moment when a client says, "I've decided to become dependent on you." No dramatic conversation where the terms of your relationship suddenly shift. Dependence creeps in quietly, politely, wearing the clothes of gratitude and appreciation.

A client thanks you a little too much. They send a quick follow-up message the next day, just to clarify something you said. Then another message a few days later, checking in. Then they're messaging before every decision, large and small, because they've started to trust your voice more than their own.

Nothing feels wrong at first. It feels like connection. It feels like you're really helping. And you are, in a way. But you're also slowly, inadvertently teaching someone that stability lives outside themselves.

Why We Become the Anchor

People come to guides during uncertainty. That's just how it works. When the ground beneath them feels shaky, they look for something solid to hold onto. A tree root. A rock. A hand reaching down.

You're that hand. You're calm when they're panicked, clear when they're confused, steady when they're falling apart. And their brain, wired for survival, does exactly what it's supposed to do: it remembers where safety came from. It attaches relief to its source. It files you away under "things that make me feel better."

This isn't weakness. It's how humans work. We seek out whatever reduced our distress before, and we seek it out again when distress returns.

The problem isn't the attachment. The problem is what happens next.

The Cycle That Traps Everyone

It goes like this:

The client feels distress. They come to you. You provide clarity. Distress decreases. Life happens, distress returns. They come back to you. You provide clarity again. Distress decreases. Repeat.

Each time, the gap between sessions shortens. Each time, they trust themselves a little less and you a little more. Each time, the pattern strengthens.

Soon, they're not coming for insight anymore. They're coming for regulation. Your presence has become the thing that steadies them, not your words. Even neutral statements bring relief because they come from you. Even silence feels safe because you're in it together.

This is the moment when guidance becomes dependence. And the guide, who never meant for any of this to happen, is now carrying something they never agreed to carry: someone else's emotional stability.

The Guide Who Couldn't Say No

I met a woman named Karen at a workshop once. She'd been practicing for about five years and had built a thriving business. Her calendar was always full. Her clients adored her. By every external measure, she was successful.

But Karen was also trapped.

She told me about one client in particular, a woman she named Diane (for privacy reasons) who'd come to her after a devastating breakup. In those early months, Diane needed extra support, and Karen gave it freely—extra time at the end of sessions, quick texts between appointments, reassurance whenever Diane's anxiety spiked.

It felt like the right thing to do. It felt compassionate.

Two years later, Diane was still messaging her multiple times a day. Still asking for reassurance about everything. Still unable to make even small decisions without Karen's input. And Karen, who'd never set a boundary because she'd never wanted to seem cold, felt like she had a second full-time job managing one person's emotional life.

"I don't know how to stop it," she told me. "She needs me. How can I just abandon her?"

But here's the hard truth Karen hadn't yet accepted: her willingness to be needed was part of what kept Diane stuck. Every text answered, every reassurance given, every boundary not set—all of it reinforced the message that Diane couldn't manage on her own. Karen's compassion had become a cage.

The Kindest Boundary

A few months after that conversation, Karen tried something different. When Diane texted with a question, Karen waited until the next morning to reply. When Diane asked for a quick call between sessions, Karen gently reminded her that they could discuss it at their next appointment. When Diane showed distress at these changes, Karen stayed calm and consistent, explaining that this was how she worked with all her clients.

The first week was rough. Diane's anxiety spiked. She sent longer messages, more urgent messages, messages asking if Karen was upset with her.

But Karen held steady.

And then something shifted. Diane started sitting with her own questions instead of immediately outsourcing them. She started making decisions without checking first. She started calling herself Karen's "graduate" instead of her client.

When I last spoke with Karen, she told me something I've never forgotten: "I thought setting boundaries would hurt her. It turns out, not setting them was what was really hurting her. I just couldn't see it because it felt so much like helping."

What Real Support Looks Like

Real support doesn't make you necessary. Real support makes yourself progressively less necessary, session by session, decision by decision, until the person sitting across from you realizes they've been holding themselves up all along.

This is hard. It's counterintuitive. Everything in us wants to be the hero, the one who saves the day, the person someone can't imagine living without. But that's not guidance. That's ego wearing compassion as a mask.

The ethical guide measures success differently. Not by how often a client returns, but by how confidently they live between visits. Not by how much they're needed, but by how well their clients function without them.

If someone becomes capable of making decisions without constant confirmation, you've succeeded—even if they never book another session. Even if they forget your name. Even if they walk away and never look back.

That's not loss. That's the whole point.

Reflections for Your Own Journey

- Do any of your clients contact you between sessions more than feels sustainable? What do they usually want?
- When someone asks you for reassurance, what do you feel—pressure, importance, responsibility? Something else?

- What habits of yours might unintentionally encourage clients to rely on you more?
- What's one boundary you could introduce that would still feel compassionate?

Chapter 5:

The Future Is Not a Promise

Sooner or later, every guide faces the question.

It comes in different forms, but the weight behind it is always the same. "Will they come back?" "Am I going to get the job?" "Is this relationship going to work out?" "Just tell me—yes or no?"

The client isn't asking for perspective. They're asking for certainty. They want you to reach into the fog of their future and pull out something solid they can hold onto. Something that will stop the spinning in their chest and let them finally, finally relax.

And here's the thing: you probably could give them something. You might even sense something real, something that later turns out to be true. The temptation to speak definitively, to offer the relief they're desperate for, is almost overwhelming.

But what happens next is rarely what either of you expects.

The Different Weight of Future Words

Imagine two kinds of information:

- Descriptive: "I'm sensing that this situation shows a pattern of hesitation and withdrawal."

- Predictive: "They will contact you within two months."

The first one helps someone understand where they are. The second one tells them where they're going. And those land very differently in the human mind.

Predictions do something powerful: they end uncertainty prematurely. The brain, which hates the discomfort of not knowing, grabs onto a predicted outcome like a lifeline. It stops exploring possibilities, stops considering alternatives, stops preparing for different scenarios. It just... waits.

Waiting feels calmer than uncertainty, yes. But waiting also suspends life. The client stops acting, stops deciding, stops participating in their own story. They become a passenger instead of a driver, watching the road for signs that your words are coming true.

You may have meant to offer comfort. You may have been trying to reduce their distress. But what you actually did was put their life on hold.

The Cost of Being Right

A guide named Patrick once told me about his most accurate prediction. A client came to him, desperate about her failing marriage. Patrick sensed strongly that the marriage would survive—that the couple would work through their difficulties and come out stronger on the other side. He told her so, with confidence.

He was right. The marriage did survive. The couple went to therapy, worked through their issues, and rebuilt their relationship.

But here's what Patrick didn't anticipate: for six months after that session, the client did nothing. She didn't suggest therapy. She didn't have hard conversations. She didn't change any of her own behaviors. She just waited, certain that everything would work out because Patrick had said so.

When the marriage finally did improve, it was despite her passivity, not because of it. And Patrick was left wondering: did I help, or did I just give her permission to stop trying?

Accuracy doesn't absolve you of responsibility. If anything, it increases it. The more confident you sound, the more someone will organize their life around your words. Being right doesn't make that okay. It just makes the impact harder to see.

The Client Who Waited Too Long

I think about a woman named Sofia who came to me years ago, worried about a health scare. She'd found a lump and was waiting for test results. She was terrified, unable to sleep or eat or focus on anything except the possibility that something was terribly wrong.

In that moment, I could have told her it would be fine. I could have sensed something—maybe I even did sense something. But instead, I said something different. I said, "I can't tell you what those results will say. What I can do is sit with you in this waiting, and help you find some ground to stand on while you're here."

She was disappointed. I could see it in her eyes. She'd come for certainty, and I'd given her presence instead.

A week later, she called me. The results had come back benign. She was fine. But that's not why she called.

"I want to thank you," she said. "That week of waiting was the hardest of my life. But something happened. I learned that I could survive not knowing. I learned that I could hold uncertainty without falling apart. If you'd told me it would be okay, I would have just waited for that to be true. Instead, I learned to wait with myself. And that changed everything."

That conversation taught me something I've never forgotten: people don't actually need certainty to survive. They need to know they can survive uncertainty.

The Honest Alternative

You don't have to refuse all future-oriented questions. You just have to answer them differently.

Instead of declaring outcomes, describe tendencies. Instead of promising events, explain influences. Instead of saying what will happen, help them understand what conditions make certain outcomes more or less likely.

"You're asking if they'll come back. I can't answer that. But I can see that communication has been blocked by hurt on both sides. If that hurt gets addressed, the dynamic could shift. If it doesn't, the distance will probably grow."

This isn't a refusal to help. It's a different kind of help—one that leaves the client in the driver's seat, equipped with understanding instead of waiting with a prediction.

What They're Really Asking

When someone demands certainty, they're rarely just asking for information. They're asking you to carry their uncertainty for them. They're saying, "This weight is too heavy. Will you hold it so I don't have to?"

If you accept, you become responsible for their emotional regulation. If you refuse harshly, they feel abandoned. The middle path is acknowledgment with steadiness. You see their fear. You understand their desire for relief. And you gently, kindly, refuse to take their weight.

"I know how much you want to know. The not-knowing is the hardest part. Let's talk about how to be with that, together."

This is the work. Not removing uncertainty, but making it survivable.

Reflections for Your Own Journey

- Think about a time you gave a strong prediction. What did the client do afterward?
- What kinds of future questions do people ask you most often?
- Try rewriting one predictive statement you commonly use into a pattern-based explanation.
- How might your sessions change if your goal became helping people act instead of helping them wait?

Chapter 6:

When the Pain Is Too Deep

There are sessions that stay with you.

Not because they were particularly profound or successful. Because they were heavy. The kind of heavy that settles into your bones and stays there, long after the client has gone home and the screen has gone dark.

I had one of those sessions years ago with a woman named Celia. She came to me three months after her son died. He was nineteen. A car accident, sudden and senseless and impossible to understand. She sat across from me, dry-eyed and hollow, and told me she didn't know why she was still getting out of bed.

In that moment, every instinct I had screamed at me to fix it. To say something profound. To offer comfort so powerful it would ease even a fraction of her pain. To be the guide who finally reached her.

But I couldn't. Because some pain can't be fixed. Some pain just has to be held.

When the Session Changes Category

Most sessions stay within a certain range. People are confused, sad, anxious, hopeful—normal human emotions, the kind we all navigate daily. Your job in those sessions is to offer perspective, clarity, maybe a little comfort around the edges.

But sometimes, the session crosses a line. The client isn't just sad; they're hopeless. Not just anxious; they're panicking. Not just confused; they're disoriented, unable to function, relying on you to tell them how to make it through the next hour.

When that happens, the session has changed categories. It's no longer guidance within normal coping range. It's crisis territory. And you, as a guide, have to shift roles—not into therapist, but into responsible boundary-holder who recognizes when something exceeds your container.

The Most Dangerous Instinct

The guides who struggle most here are the ones with the biggest hearts. They feel that if they don't go deeper, they're abandoning the person. They believe their presence is uniquely healing, that the client chose them for a reason, that they'd be cruel to refer out when the client finally feels safe enough to open up.

So they stay longer. They answer late-night messages. They try to manage the person's emotional state themselves, session after session, until they're carrying a weight no single person should carry alone.

This isn't compassion. It's a slow-motion disaster.

Crisis requires systems that spiritual guidance doesn't provide—continuous monitoring, safety assessment, trained intervention, backup support. When you try to be all of those things for someone, you're not helping them. You're becoming a substitute for real help, and both of you will eventually pay the price.

The Woman Who Needed More

I learned this lesson from a guide named Teresa, who'd been practicing for about eight years when she took on a client named James. James had a history of trauma, deep and complex, that he'd never properly addressed. He came to Teresa for "spiritual support" and quickly became one of her most devoted clients.

They met weekly. Then twice weekly. Then James started messaging between sessions, sometimes multiple times a day. He told Teresa she was the only one who understood him, the only one who'd ever really seen him. She felt honored, chosen, uniquely qualified to help.

Eight months in, James had a breakdown. He stopped eating, stopped sleeping, stopped being able to work. He called Teresa fourteen times in one night, begging her to tell him what to do, how to survive, how to make the pain stop.

Teresa was in over her head and she knew it. But she also felt responsible. She'd been his primary support for almost a year. How could she abandon him now?

It took another three months, a crisis team, and a lot of painful conversations before James finally got the specialized help he'd needed all along. And it took Teresa years to forgive herself for not seeing sooner that her care, however genuine, had become part of the problem.

What Real Help Looks Like in Crisis

When crisis shows up, your job changes. You become two things: a stabilizer and a connector.

Stabilizer means you stay calm. You don't panic. You don't escalate. Your voice remains steady, your presence grounded, even when what you're hearing terrifies you. You model the possibility of being with pain without being consumed by it.

Connector means you guide them toward appropriate support. Not because you're rejecting them, but because you're taking their pain seriously enough to ensure they get what they actually need.

"James, what you're describing is so heavy. I'm glad you trusted me with it. And I also know that this is beyond what I'm equipped to hold. Let me help you find someone who has the training to walk with you through this part."

This isn't abandonment. This is the most responsible form of care. You're not saying "go away." You're saying "you deserve more than I can give."

The Grief That Can't Be Fixed

Celia, the woman who lost her son, taught me something about holding space without fixing.

I didn't try to make her feel better. I didn't offer spiritual explanations about why her son died. I didn't tell her he was in a better place or that she'd see him again. I just sat with her, week after week, and let her be exactly where she was.

Sometimes she cried. Sometimes she raged. Sometimes she sat in silence, staring at nothing, while I held the quiet with her. Sometimes she asked questions I couldn't answer—why him, why now, why anything—and I said, "I don't know. That's so hard, not knowing."

A year later, she told me something I've never forgotten. "Everyone wanted to fix me. They wanted me to move on, for me to heal, for me to find meaning. You were the only one who just let me be broken. And somehow, that's what let me start putting pieces back together."

Not all pain needs to be resolved. Some just needs to be witnessed. And knowing the difference—between pain you can help with and pain you can only hold—is one of the most important skills a guide can develop.

The Signs That You're Over Your Depth

You're no longer in a standard session when the client:

- Can't describe basic coping strategies
- Talks about not wanting to go on
- Seems to be escalating instead of calming down
- Asks you to tell them how to live moment to moment
- Treats you as their only source of stability

You may also notice your own internal signals: you feel responsible for their safety, you dread ending sessions, you worry about what happens after they leave. Your anxiety here isn't spiritual insight. It's ethical awareness knocking on your door.

Listen to it.

Reflections for Your Own Journey

- Have you ever kept a session going longer than you should have because the client seemed too fragile to stop? What made it hard to end?
- When someone shares really heavy experiences with you, what do you feel—urgency, responsibility, fear, pressure?
- Write a sentence you could say to a client that would guide them toward additional support without making them feel dismissed.
- What local or online resources could you learn about now, so you're prepared if crisis shows up?

Chapter 7:

The Honest Conversation About Money

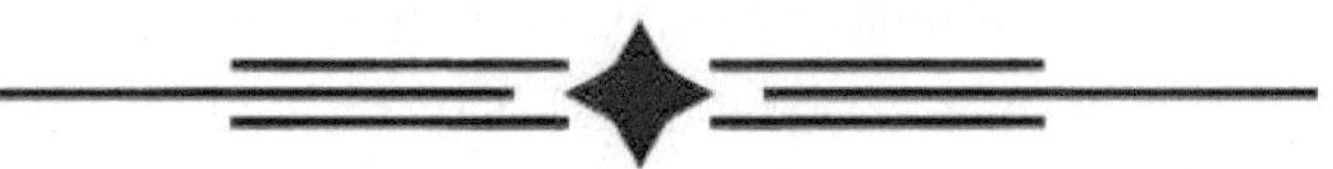

Money makes everyone uncomfortable.

Not all the time, and not in every context. But put money and spiritual guidance in the same room, and suddenly the air gets thick with unspoken questions. Is it okay to charge for this? Am I being greedy? Will people think I'm only in it for the money? Shouldn't this work be freely given?

I've wrestled with these questions myself, for years. And here's what I've come to understand: money isn't the problem. Unclear money is the problem. Money without structure, money without boundaries, money that floats around unexamined while expectations pile up on both sides—that's what causes the trouble.

The Two Traps Guides Fall Into

Most guides, when they start charging, fall into one of two patterns.

The Over-Giver

They feel guilty taking payment for something that feels natural, even effortless. So they lower their prices. They extend sessions.

They throw in free follow-ups. They avoid enforcing policies because it feels transactional.

Inside, they're thinking: "I don't want them to feel like I'm just doing this for money."

Clients appreciate this generosity at first. Then they get confused. What are they actually paying for? Time? Access? Emotional availability? The rules aren't clear, so they start testing boundaries, pushing limits, asking for more.

Eventually, the over-giver feels drained, resentful, and deeply unappreciated. They gave everything and got exhaustion in return.

The Defensive Charger

They're afraid of being taken advantage of. So they put up walls. They become rigid, transactional, emotionally distant. They hide behind policies and protect themselves from connection.

Inside, they're thinking: "If I care too much, they'll expect too much."

Clients may respect their boundaries, but they feel no warmth, no real contact. The sessions are professional but hollow. The guide feels safe but empty, protected from burnout but also cut off from the very thing that drew them to this work.

Neither extreme works. The path lies somewhere in between: clear compensation delivered with steady care.

The Woman Who Charged Nothing

I knew a guide named Patricia who refused to charge for her work. She was deeply intuitive, genuinely gifted, and completely convinced that money would corrupt her gift. She took donations sometimes, if people insisted, but never set a price. Never asked for anything specific in return.

At first, this felt beautiful. People flocked to her. Her calendar was always full. She felt like she was living her purpose, giving freely from an endless well.

Three years in, Patricia was broke, exhausted, and secretly resenting every client who walked through her door. She'd see someone's name on her calendar and feel a flash of irritation instead of welcome. She'd rush through sessions, eager to get to the next thing, the next person, the next demand on her dwindling energy.

"You know what the worst part is?" she told me once. "I can't even be honest about it. I'm the one who chose to work for free. I'm the one who set this up. So now I just have to pretend I'm grateful while I'm slowly dying inside."

Patricia's gift hadn't been corrupted by money. It had been destroyed by its absence. Without the structure that payment provides—the clear exchange, the defined container, the visible edges of the transaction—her work had expanded to fill her entire life. And there was nothing left for her.

What Payment Actually Does

Payment does more than compensate you. It organizes the interaction in the client's mind.

Free conversations feel optional. They're gifts, appreciated but not weighted. Paid sessions feel intentional. When someone invests money, they pay attention differently. They prepare more carefully. They listen more actively. They remember more accurately.

Payment increases engagement.

But only if the edges are clear. If the client pays yet still receives unlimited access, their brain can't categorize the experience. Confusion forms: Am I paying for time? For answers? For ongoing support? This confusion becomes the root of most disputes.

The Client Who Needed to Pay

I worked with a man named Robert years ago who initially refused to let me work for free. He was wealthy, successful, accustomed to paying for expertise. When I suggested a reduced rate because he was going through a hard time, he looked almost offended.

"With respect," he said, "I need to pay you. If I don't pay, this is just a conversation. If I pay, it's a commitment. I'll show up differently. I'll listen differently. I'll actually do the work instead of just talking about it."

He was right. The money wasn't for me. It was for him—a container that held his attention, his intention, his willingness to engage. By paying, he was investing in his own process. By letting him pay, I was honoring that investment.

The Inner Work of Pricing

Pricing isn't just about what the market will bear. It's about what you need to stay sustainable. It's about the energy you expend, the focus you maintain, the weight you carry. It's about being able to show up fully for one client after another without draining yourself dry.

Your price should reflect:

- The time a session takes
- The mental focus required
- The emotional load you carry
- The experience you've developed
- The responsibility you assume

When your price aligns with all of that, something shifts. You stop feeling guilty. You stop over-giving to compensate. You stop resenting clients for existing. You just... work. Cleanly, clearly, sustainably.

And clients sense that. They feel the solidity of someone who values their own work. They trust you more, not less, because you've drawn a clear line around what you offer.

Reflections for Your Own Journey

- What do you feel when you state your price—confidence, apology, hesitation? Be honest.
- Have you ever extended a session or added free follow-up because you felt your fee was too high or too low?
- Write a simple description of what a client receives from you. Use no symbolic language—just concrete details.
- What would change in your practice if your pricing fully matched the effort you give?

Chapter 8:

You're Not Just Helping—You're Running Something

Some words make guides uncomfortable. Business is one of them. It sounds corporate, cold, disconnected from the sacred work of guiding others. It sounds like spreadsheets and profit margins and everything we're trying to escape by doing this work in the first place.

I understand that discomfort. I felt it too, for years.

But here's what I've learned: refusing to call it a business doesn't make it not a business. It just makes it a messy business, one without clear edges, where expectations collide and boundaries blur and everyone ends up confused about what's actually being offered.

When strangers pay you regularly for a service, you're operating a business. Whether you call it that or not. And the sooner you accept this, the easier everything becomes.

What a Business Actually Does

Think about what a business provides:

- Predictability: people know what to expect
- Clarity: the offer is visible and understandable
- Repeatability: the same quality, session after session
- Fairness: everyone gets the same container

All of these things reduce misunderstanding. All of them protect relationships. All of them make it easier for clients to trust you, because they don't have to guess how things work.

Informality feels kind in the moment. Structure feels kind over time. A business doesn't remove heart from your work. It protects heart from chaos.

The Guide Who Didn't Want a Business

I once mentored a woman named Lena who was brilliant at her work. Clients loved her. She had a waiting list and more referrals than she could handle. By every measure, she was successful.

But Lena was also drowning. Her booking system was a mess—people emailed her directly, and she manually scheduled them in a paper calendar. Her policies existed only in her head, so she had to explain them to every new client individually. Her follow-up communication was inconsistent, varying wildly depending on her energy level that day.

"I don't want to be a business," she told me. "I just want to help people."

"Lena," I said gently, "you're already a business. You just have a really inefficient, exhausting one."

We spent the next few months building systems. A real website with clear descriptions. An online booking calendar. Written policies that lived on her site instead of in her explanations. A simple email template for follow-ups.

The first week after launching, Lena called me, almost in tears. "I have so much more energy," she said. "I'm not answering the same questions over and over. People show up already knowing how things work. I actually look forward to sessions again."

The business hadn't drained her work of meaning. It had given her work a container strong enough to hold its weight.

What Makes Something a Practice

A practice exists when the experience can be understood without your explanation. A new client should know what happens, how long it lasts, what to expect afterward, before they ever speak to you.

If they have to message you to learn how your service works, your structure exists only in your mind. It's not real yet. It's just ideas you carry around, invisible to everyone else.

Your practice becomes real the day a stranger can engage with it without needing a conversation first. The day your website, your policies, your process explain everything clearly enough that people can decide whether you're right for them without asking you a single question.

That's when you've built something that can grow without draining you.

The Four Things Every Practice Needs

Every sustainable practice rests on four visible elements:

Description: What exactly do you offer? Be specific. "Intuitive guidance" means different things to different people. "A 60-minute session exploring patterns in your relationships" means the same thing to everyone.

Process: How does it unfold? People relax when they know what comes next. Beginning, middle, ending—make them visible so clients can stop guessing and start participating.

Boundaries: What's outside your scope? Clients don't mind limits they knew about in advance. They mind limits they discover after emotional investment.

Records: What gets remembered? Memory is unreliable. Simple documentation protects everyone when details get fuzzy months later.

These four things don't make you cold. They make you clear. And clarity is the foundation of trust.

The Emotional Relief of Systems

The most surprising thing about building systems is how good they feel. Not just for clients—for you.

You stop deciding everything repeatedly. You stop worrying about forgetting promises. You stop feeling pressured to respond instantly. Decisions move from emotion to procedure, from "what feels right right now" to "this is how we do things."

This frees up enormous mental energy. Energy you can use for the actual work—listening, interpreting, being present—instead of managing logistics and negotiating boundaries in real time.

Systems don't drain your work of life. They give your work room to breathe.

Reflections for Your Own Journey

- If a stranger visited your website today, would they know exactly how a session works without asking you?
- What part of your process currently depends on you explaining it individually to each client?
- Which boundary do you most often enforce verbally instead of having it visible beforehand?
- What's one simple system you could introduce this week that would reduce the number of decisions you have to make?

Chapter 9:

The Agreement That Protects You Both

Most guides avoid written agreements.

Not because they're lazy or disorganized. Because agreements feel like distrust. They feel like preparing for failure, anticipating conflict, assuming the worst about people who come to you in vulnerable states.

I felt that way too, for years. I thought my kindness, my willingness to explain things verbally, my commitment to being reasonable—I thought all of that would be enough. I thought good intentions could substitute for clear terms.

I was wrong.

The Invisible Expectations Problem

Before every session, two people arrive with different pictures in their heads.

The client imagines answers, reassurance, clarity, maybe ongoing support. The guide intends interpretation, perspective, a time-limited interaction with defined scope. Neither is wrong. Neither is unreasonable. But neither has checked their picture against the other's.

From a legal perspective a contract is formed when there are two parties that have a "meeting of the minds" about what is being offered and what is being accepted. The challenge, many times, is that there is ambiguity about what was truly being offered by the service. The spiritual services provider has the responsibility to ensure that the offer is very clear and precise so the client is not left with a different understanding of what to expect.

During the session, the client hears everything through their lens. After the session, they evaluate the experience through that same lens. If the pictures never got compared, satisfaction depends on luck.

An agreement replaces luck with clarity.

Why Verbal Explanations Aren't Enough

You can explain everything beforehand. You can be clear, thorough, patient. You can cover every detail and answer every question.

And the client, who is anxious, grieving, preoccupied, or desperate, will hear maybe half of it. Their brain, focused on relief, filters out everything that doesn't reduce tension. They hear the parts that comfort them and forget the parts that limit them.

Days or weeks later, they remember the emotional experience but not the procedural explanation. You remember explaining. They remember understanding differently. And suddenly you're in conflict over something you both could have sworn was clear.

Written terms create shared memory. They give both of you something to return to when recollection diverges.

The Client Who Remembered Differently

A guide named Daniel learned this the hard way. He had a session with a woman named Maria, who was devastated about a recent breakup. Daniel was compassionate, present, and careful. At the end, Maria thanked him profusely and said she'd be in touch.

Three months later, Daniel got a chargeback notification from his payment processor. Maria had disputed the charge, claiming Daniel promised her that her ex would return within two months, and when that didn't happen, she felt cheated.

Daniel was stunned. He remembered the session clearly. He'd been careful not to make any promises. He'd talked about patterns and possibilities, never certainties. But he had no record of what he'd actually said, no documentation to counter Maria's memory of events.

The chargeback went through. Daniel lost the money and, worse, lost trust in his own memory. He started recording sessions after that, but the damage was done. A simple written agreement, reviewed and signed beforehand, could have prevented everything.

What an Agreement Actually Does

A good agreement accomplishes four things:

It defines the role: "I provide perspective and interpretation. I do not predict specific outcomes."

It defines the limits: "Sessions last 60 minutes. Follow-up communication is for scheduling only."

It defines responsibility: "You make your own decisions. I am not responsible for outcomes that follow from our conversations."

It defines the interaction: "Here's how booking works, here's how cancellation works, here's what happens between sessions."

Once these are visible, the client stops having to guess. They don't have to wonder whether it's okay to message you at midnight. They don't have to interpret your silence as rejection. They don't have to read between the lines for hidden meanings.

Everything is right there, in writing, agreed to by both of you before the work begins.

The Guide Who Feared Written Terms

I worked with a guide named Simone who resisted written agreements for years. She worried they'd make her feel like a lawyer instead of a healer. She worried clients would feel distrusted, distanced, turned into transactions instead of people.

But after one too many misunderstandings—a client who expected weekly check-ins, another who demanded a refund because she "didn't feel better," a third who kept messaging months after their last session—Simone finally gave in.

She drafted a simple one-page agreement. Nothing legalistic, just clear statements about what she offered and what she didn't. She started sending it to every new client before their first session.

The first month, three people declined to book. They wanted guarantees, ongoing access, someone to hold their hand indefinitely. Simone felt a pang of loss—and then relief. Those weren't her people. They never had been. The agreement had just made that visible sooner.

The clients who did book arrived differently. More prepared. More respectful. More ready to actually work instead of just receive. Simone's practice didn't shrink; it got better. And she stopped spending energy managing people who weren't a good fit in the first place.

The Peace of Mind You Can't Buy

Perhaps the greatest benefit of written agreements is internal. You stop wondering what's fair case by case. You stop adjusting boundaries based on mood or guilt. You stop carrying conversations in your head after they end.

The structure holds everything. You just show up and do the work.

This doesn't make you cold. It makes you sustainable. And sustainability is the most caring thing you can offer, because it means you'll still be here, clear and present, for everyone who needs you next.

Reflections for Your Own Journey

- List three misunderstandings you've had with clients. What assumption caused each one?
- Which boundary do you currently explain most often out loud?
- Write one sentence that describes your role in a session—just the role, nothing else.
- What would change emotionally for you if expectations were written down before every session?

Chapter 10:

What Happens Outside the Session Matters Most

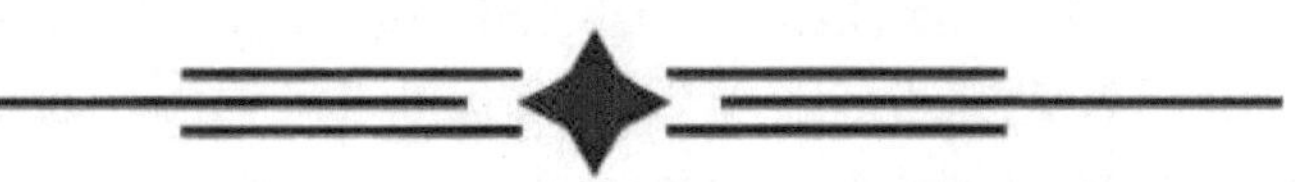

Most of this book has been about what happens inside sessions. The conversations, the boundaries, the careful dance of guidance and support.

But here's something I've learned the hard way: the greatest risks to a practice rarely come from sessions themselves. They come from what happens afterward—in messages, in memory, in the public spaces where sessions get discussed without your presence.

A single sentence, quoted out of context, can outweigh hundreds of helpful conversations. Not because your work lacks value, but because perception spreads faster than context. And once something is out there, you can't pull it back.

The Illusion of Private Conversations

We treat sessions as confidential because they feel intimate. Two people, talking deeply, sharing openly. Of course it's private. Of course it stays between us.

But modern communication has changed what privacy means. Screenshots exist. Messages can be saved. Statements can be repeated without tone, without context, without any of the warmth or nuance that accompanied them originally.

You can conduct a thoughtful, careful session, and a single sentence, repeated alone, can sound completely different to someone who wasn't there. Not because the client is malicious, but because humans process by sharing. They tell friends what you said. They post about it online. They ask others whether it sounds right.

Once that happens, your words belong to the world. And the world interprets them without you.

Why Clients Share

Most clients don't share to hurt you. They share because they're processing.

They're trying to make sense of what you said, to integrate it into their understanding, to check whether it resonates with people they trust. Your words become part of a broader conversation, one that continues long after your session ends.

This is normal. It's human. It doesn't mean you should stop being honest or careful. It just means you should be aware that your words have a life beyond the room where you speak them.

The Guide Who Was Quoted

I knew a guide named Rachel who had a single sentence from a session posted online. The client, who'd been going through a painful divorce, shared one thing Rachel said: "Sometimes people leave because they're supposed to."

Out of context, it sounded cold. Dismissive. Like Rachel was minimizing years of marriage and shared history. The post got shared, and shared again, and soon people who'd never met Rachel were calling her cruel and unfeeling.

What the post didn't include was the rest of the session. The hour of tears that came before that sentence. The careful exploration of patterns that led up to it. The way Rachel held space for grief even while naming a possibility. None of that traveled with the quote.

Rachel spent weeks trying to explain, to add context, to defend herself. It didn't work. The damage was done, not because she'd done anything wrong, but because a single sentence, alone, had become the whole story.

What You Can Control

You can't control what clients share. You can't control how your words get repeated. You can't control the context that gets lost in translation.

What you can control is your own consistency. Your own calm. Your own response when things go sideways.

If you're criticized publicly, your instinct will be to explain, to correct, to defend. But public conversations rarely resolve through detail. They resolve through tone. A calm, steady response—acknowledging the person's experience without arguing interpretation—speaks louder than any defense.

Observers aren't evaluating the original session. They're evaluating your composure. Your response becomes part of your professional identity, whether you want it to or not.

The Power of Not Engaging

Sometimes the most powerful response is no response.

Not every criticism needs a rebuttal. Not every misrepresentation needs correction. Some things just need to be let go, allowed to pass, absorbed by the sheer weight of your ongoing consistency.

A stable practice is defined more by patterns than by isolated events. One negative post, one misunderstood session, one angry client—these things matter less than the hundreds of ordinary interactions where you showed up, did the work, and helped someone.

Knowing when not to engage protects your energy and your reputation simultaneously.

The Documentation That Saves You

Simple records—dates, duration, general focus—provide clarity when memory diverges. Not detailed notes that invade privacy, just enough to ground a conversation if questions arise months later.

A client once contacted me a year after our last session, asking about something she thought I'd promised. I didn't remember promising anything, but I also didn't trust my memory. So I checked my notes: date, duration, topics discussed. Nothing about a promise.

I was able to respond calmly: "I don't have any record of that in my notes, and it's not something I typically offer. Can you tell me more about what you remember?"

The conversation stayed grounded. We weren't arguing about who was right. We were comparing recollections, anchored by documentation. It never escalated because there was nothing to escalate.

Documentation isn't distrust. It's clarity preserved.

Reflections for Your Own Journey

- What parts of your communication currently happen in casual messages that could benefit from more structure?
- How would you respond calmly if someone publicly misunderstood something you said?
- What personal information do you share that isn't necessary for your service?
- What simple documentation habit could you start this week?

Chapter 11:

Why Boundaries Actually Build Trust

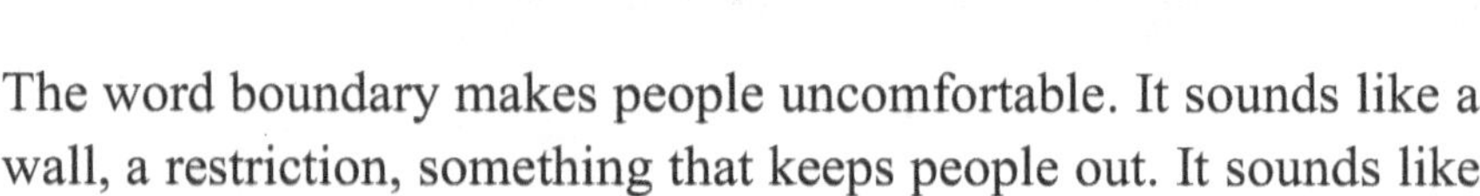

The word boundary makes people uncomfortable. It sounds like a wall, a restriction, something that keeps people out. It sounds like the opposite of connection, the enemy of intimacy.

But here's what I've learned after years of doing this work: boundaries don't reduce trust. They create the conditions for trust to exist.

Imagine walking into a room where the floor keeps shifting. Where the walls move unpredictably. Where the ceiling sometimes lowers and sometimes rises. You wouldn't relax there, no matter how beautifully decorated it was. You'd stay alert, vigilant, unable to settle because you never knew what would happen next.

That's what it feels like to work with someone whose boundaries are unclear. The warmth might be there, the care might be genuine, but the instability makes real trust impossible.

Why Humans Need Edges

Every meaningful relationship depends on predictability. And predictability requires visible edges.

When your availability is consistent, clients stop wondering when they can reach you. When session length is consistent, they stop watching the clock. When your responses are consistent, they stop reading between the lines for hidden meanings.

Consistency creates safety. And boundaries are the visible edges of consistency.

The Anxiety of Unlimited Access

Unlimited access sounds generous. It feels like you're giving everything, holding nothing back, offering yourself fully to everyone who needs you.

But to the client, it often feels confusing. They wonder: Is it okay to reach out again? Am I bothering them? Should I wait for them to contact me? Did I do something wrong when they didn't respond?

The guide thinks they're being supportive. The client feels unsure how to interact. Both people are trying their best, and both end up anxious.

Clear limits remove social guesswork. When communication has defined channels and times, clients don't worry about crossing invisible lines. They engage confidently because expectations are shared. Freedom exists inside structure.

The Client Who Needed Limits

I worked with a woman named Grace who initially struggled with boundaries. She'd been to guides before who were always available, always responsive, always happy to chat between sessions. When she started with me, she expected the same.

The first time she messaged with a non-urgent question, I didn't respond until the next morning. The second time, I gently reminded her that we could discuss things fully in our next session. The third time, I didn't respond at all—just brought it up when we met.

Grace was frustrated at first. She told me she felt dismissed, like I didn't care as much as her previous guides.

But something shifted over time. She started bringing better questions to sessions, more thoughtful and prepared. She started sitting with her own confusion instead of immediately outsourcing it. She started trusting her own judgment more.

Near the end of our work together, she said something I've never forgotten: "I used to think the guides who were always available were the caring ones. Now I realize they were just keeping me small. You were the first one who trusted me enough to let me struggle."

The Respect Effect

Something surprising happens when you enforce consistent limits: respect increases.

Not because clients enjoy restrictions, but because limits signal professionalism. People trust those who appear capable of sustaining their work. A guide who protects their time and energy seems stable. A guide who's always available seems like they might burn out at any moment.

Stability attracts confidence. Clients may notice the boundary at first. Soon, they notice the reliability behind it.

When Clients Push Back

Occasionally, someone will react strongly to a new boundary. They'll express hurt, frustration, even anger. They'll tell you you've changed, that you used to be more available, that you don't care as much anymore.

This reaction isn't proof the boundary is wrong. It's proof the previous expectation was different. Humans adapt to new structures, but adaptation takes time. Most resistance occurs during transition, not afterward.

If you hold steady—calmly, consistently, without apology—the relationship usually stabilizes at a healthier level. If you give in, you reset expectations and prolong the discomfort.

Consistency communicates seriousness.

The Guide Who Couldn't Hold the Line

A guide named Valerie once told me about a client who'd been with her for years. They'd grown close over time, their sessions blurring into something that felt more like friendship than professional guidance. Valerie answered late-night messages, extended sessions, shared personal details.

When Valerie tried to pull back—to enforce the boundaries she'd never established—her client reacted with fury. Accusations flew. Old confidences were weaponized. The relationship ended badly, with hurt on both sides and damage that took Valerie years to fully process.

"It's my fault," she told me afterward. "I taught her that the rules didn't apply. I let her believe our relationship was something other than what it was. When I tried to change it, she felt betrayed. And she was right to feel that way. I just didn't see it coming."

Boundaries established late feel like punishment. Boundaries established early feel like structure. The difference is everything.

The Calm Delivery of Limits

How you present a boundary matters as much as the boundary itself.

Apologetic delivery suggests the rule is negotiable. Defensive delivery suggests conflict. Calm delivery suggests normalcy—this is just how things work, nothing personal, nothing unusual.

When you present limits as standard procedure, clients accept them as part of the experience. Your tone teaches them how to feel about the structure. If you're relaxed, they relax. If you're tense, they get tense.

Neutrality preserves dignity for everyone.

Reflections for Your Own Journey

- Which boundary do you most often hesitate to enforce?

- When you imagine setting it consistently, what concern arises?
- Write one sentence explaining that boundary calmly and neutrally.
- How might your sessions improve if both you and your client knew exactly where they begin and end?

Chapter 12:

The Quiet Science of Being Trusted

Many guides believe trust comes from being impressive. From saying the right thing at the right time. From having insights so profound that clients can't help but believe.

But here's what I've observed after years in this work: trust has almost nothing to do with being impressive. It has everything to do with being predictable.

Before a client decides whether your words are accurate, they decide whether your presence feels stable. They evaluate safety first, truth second. And safety comes from consistency, not brilliance.

How the Mind Decides

Human beings trust through pattern recognition, not logical proof. The brain quietly asks: Is this person the same every time? Do they react predictably? Can I anticipate how this interaction will unfold?

If the answer is yes, the mind relaxes and opens. If the answer is no, the mind stays cautious, vigilant, evaluating instead of receiving.

This is why a calm guide who speaks carefully often appears more credible than an expressive one who speaks dramatically. Consistency communicates safety faster than intensity communicates confidence.

The Four Signals

Clients unconsciously look for four things during early interactions. When these are present, trust grows almost automatically.

Structured Process

When sessions follow a clear flow, clients know where they are in the interaction. They stop wondering what comes next and start focusing on themselves. Predictability reduces vigilance. Clarity frees attention.

Emotional Steadiness

Neutrality doesn't mean indifference. It means your reactions remain proportionate. If you seem shocked by small things or overly certain about complex ones, the client senses instability. When your tone stays measured, they feel safe sharing honestly.

Consistent Boundaries

A guide who enforces limits kindly but firmly appears grounded. A guide who adjusts rules frequently appears uncertain. The mind trusts those who operate the same way repeatedly.

Clear Language

Language that avoids exaggeration feels more accurate. The brain associates careful wording with thoughtful reasoning. Dramatic phrasing creates short-term impact but long-term doubt. Measured phrasing creates lasting confidence.

The Guide Who Was Too Exciting

I once knew a guide named Marcus who was electrifying to watch. His readings were dramatic, full of bold predictions and mystical language. Clients left his sessions buzzing, amazed, convinced they'd encountered someone truly special.

But Marcus's clients rarely stayed. They'd come for the experience, get their emotional hit, and then drift away, looking for the next amazing thing. Those who did stay became dependent on the drama, needing bigger and bigger experiences to feel the same charge.

Marcus was popular but not trusted. People loved watching him, but they didn't rely on him. When things got hard, they went somewhere else—somewhere steadier, quieter, more predictable.

The Guide Who Was Just Present

Another guide, a woman named Helen, worked very differently. She didn't make predictions. She didn't use mystical language. She just sat with people, listened carefully, and reflected back what she heard in plain, simple words.

Nothing about her sessions was dramatic. Clients didn't leave buzzing with excitement. They left thoughtful, reflective, sometimes challenged. They left with questions to ponder, not answers to hold.

But Helen's clients stayed. Years later, they were still coming back—not for drama, but for clarity. They trusted her because she was the same person every time. Same presence. Same attention. Same calm.

Helen's trust wasn't built on being impressive. It was built on being reliable. And reliability outlasts excitement every time.

The Role of Silence

One of the strongest signals of authority is not speaking immediately.

Silence communicates thoughtfulness. It tells the client you're processing, not reacting. It gives their words room to land, to matter, to be held.

Rapid responses feel attentive but can seem automatic. Measured pauses suggest consideration. People trust answers that appear formed, not just produced.

Your pace communicates intention.

Why Less Is More

When guides feel pressure to prove themselves, they often add more—more explanation, more insight, more certainty. But excessive explanation weakens credibility. It sounds like justification, not clarity.

Simple statements appear confident. Long defenses sound uncertain. Authority rarely requires convincing. It requires stating observations and letting them stand.

The most trusted guides say less, not more. They trust their words to carry their own weight.

Reflections for Your Own Journey

- When you feel pressure to sound convincing, how does your speech change?
- What part of your process currently varies most between sessions?
- Practice stating one observation in a single sentence, without adding any justification.
- How might your presence change if your goal became steadiness instead of impressiveness?

Chapter 13:

Becoming Someone People Know

At the beginning, recognition feels like a visibility problem. You think about platforms and algorithms and reaching more people. You worry about being seen, being heard, being found by those who need you.

But over time, you realize something: attention and recognition are not the same thing.

Attention is when many people see you. Recognition is when people know what to expect from you. One produces temporary growth. The other produces a lasting practice.

The Difference Between Audience and Reputation

An audience reacts to content. A reputation responds to experience.

An audience may follow you for entertainment, curiosity, or interest. A reputation forms when someone confidently refers another person because they understand what you consistently provide.

Recognition begins the moment a client says: "You should talk to them. They're steady."

Not exciting. Not dramatic. Steady.

Reliability spreads more quietly than excitement, but it spreads farther because it carries responsibility. People don't recommend professionals casually. They protect their own credibility when suggesting you. Your authority grows when others risk their trust on your consistency.

The Guide Who Wanted to Be Known

A guide named Phillip spent years trying to build his audience. He posted constantly, engaged everywhere, showed up in every space where potential clients might gather. He was visible, active, undeniably present.

But something was missing. People knew his name, but they didn't know his work. They'd seen his posts, but they couldn't describe what he actually did. His visibility hadn't translated into recognition.

When Phillip finally stopped trying to be everywhere and started focusing on clarity—on defining his role, his process, his specific offer—something shifted. The people who found him understood him immediately. They didn't need explanations because his purpose was visible from the start.

His audience shrank. His practice grew. Recognition had finally arrived.

The Power of Simplicity

Every recognized guide has a signature—not a mystical style, but a clear function. Someone should be able to describe your work in one sentence. Not your personality. Not your beliefs. Your role.

"They help people understand relationship patterns so they can make clearer choices."

"They offer perspective on career decisions using intuitive insights."

"They support people through grief by creating space for whatever arises."

When your role is that clear, recognition becomes inevitable. People know what to expect. They know who to send. They know how to describe you to others.

The Referral That Means Most

Referrals are the truest marker of recognition. Not because they bring business, but because they carry trust.

A referred client arrives differently. They listen sooner. They question less. They prepare more carefully. Because someone they trust has already evaluated you. Someone has staked their own credibility on your reliability.

Referrals happen not when clients feel amazed, but when they feel safe recommending you without concern. When they trust your predictability, not your drama.

The Long Path

Recognition rarely grows linearly. You may experience periods of increased visibility without increased recognition. Many people know you exist, but few understand your role.

Then gradually, after repeated consistent experiences, referrals increase quietly. New clients arrive who already understand your boundaries and process before meeting you. They've heard about you from someone who trusted you, and they come with that trust already extended.

Recognition has begun. It appears slower because it's deeper.

The Guide Who Waited

I think about a guide named Margaret who worked quietly for fifteen years before anyone outside her immediate community knew her name. She didn't post on social media. She didn't have a website for the first decade. She just worked, session after session, building trust one person at a time.

When I met her, she had a waiting list eighteen months long. People flew across the country to see her. She'd never advertised, never promoted, never tried to be visible. Her reputation had spread entirely through word of mouth, carried by clients who knew exactly what she offered and trusted her completely.

"That's the only kind of recognition that matters," she told me. "When someone sends their friend to you, they're sending a piece of themselves. They're trusting you with someone they love. That's not something you can buy with marketing."

She was right. Recognition isn't about being known. It's about being known for something—something clear, something reliable, something worth trusting.

Reflections for Your Own Journey

- In one sentence, how would a current client describe your service?
- What part of your work changes most depending on who books?
- Are your public explanations consistent with what actually happens in sessions?
- What would become simpler if your role were more specific?

Chapter 14:

When You Have to Let Someone Go

No matter how clear, consistent, and careful you are, you will eventually encounter someone who doesn't fit within the healthy rhythm of your practice.

Not someone who simply asks questions. Someone who can't stop asking. Someone who messages constantly, reinterprets your words obsessively, seeks reassurance faster than you can give it. Someone who treats your presence as the only thing keeping them steady.

These clients aren't bad people. They're struggling people. And their struggle can pull you into a dynamic that helps no one.

What "Difficult" Really Looks Like

Difficult doesn't always mean confrontational. Some of the most challenging clients are the most grateful, the most appreciative, the most devoted. Their difficulty lies not in what they demand, but in how they attach.

Common patterns include:

- Asking for confirmation repeatedly, about the same things
- Getting more emotional after each answer instead of less
- Booking session after session without integrating anything between them
- Interpreting neutral statements as personal reassurance
- Assuming a personal relationship exists beyond the professional one

The guide feels pulled to stabilize rather than guide. The session shifts from interpretive work to emotional regulation. And both people get stuck in a cycle that neither intended.

Why Obsession Forms

Obsession is rarely about the guide personally. It's about certainty.

When someone experiences unresolved emotional tension—especially around relationships, loss, or major life decisions—their mind searches for a fixed point. Something solid to hold onto in the chaos. You become that point. Not because you claimed it, but because you remained calm while they felt unstable.

The brain associates relief with your presence. Instead of processing internally, they seek contact externally. Each reassurance reduces anxiety briefly. Brief relief reinforces repeated contact.

The cycle strengthens itself.

The Guide Who Couldn't Let Go

I worked with a guide named Tamara who had a client named Joel. Joel had been abandoned by his parents as a child and carried wounds that never fully healed. In Tamara, he found someone who listened, who stayed, who didn't leave. He became devoted to her in a way that felt flattering at first.

But Joel's devotion had no limits. He messaged constantly. He sent gifts. He talked about Tamara to everyone he knew as the person who saved his life. When Tamara didn't respond quickly enough, he spiraled into anxiety and self-doubt.

Tamara felt trapped. She cared about Joel. She didn't want to hurt him. But she also felt suffocated, responsible, unable to live her own life without managing his reactions.

"Every time my phone buzzes, I hope it's not him," she told me. "And then I feel terrible for hoping that. He needs me. How can I resent someone who needs me?"

What Tamara hadn't yet accepted was that her continued availability was part of what kept Joel stuck. Every response reinforced the message that stability lived outside him. Every reassurance taught him to come to her first. Her compassion had become a cage for both of them.

The First Step: Clarification

Before disengaging, clarify structure.

Restate communication expectations. Reinforce session-based interaction. Encourage time between appointments. Do this calmly, neutrally, without apology—not as a correction, but as a reminder of how things work.

Many clients adjust once the pattern becomes visible. They didn't realize they'd been overreaching. They didn't notice how dependent they'd become. Your clarity gives them a chance to recalibrate.

When Adjustment Doesn't Happen

Some clients can't adapt because their need isn't guidance—it's regulation. More sessions don't resolve the cycle. They just shorten it. Relief becomes briefer after each contact.

At this point, ethical practice requires reducing reinforcement. Not withdrawing care, but preventing deeper dependency.

You increase response intervals. You limit communication to scheduled sessions. You encourage additional support systems. Your presence remains respectful but no longer immediate.

The client begins redirecting regulation elsewhere. Ideally, toward healthier structures.

The Client Who Needed to Go

Tamara eventually had to end her work with Joel. It was one of the hardest conversations she'd ever had.

"Joel, I need to be honest with you. The way we're working together isn't helping you as much as it should. You've come to rely on me in a way that keeps you from relying on yourself. I think you need someone who can offer more than I can—someone trained to work with the depth of what you're carrying."

Joel was devastated. He accused Tamara of abandoning him, of not caring, of being just like everyone else who'd left. Tamara held steady, calm, not defending or explaining. She just kept returning to the same message: "I care about you. That's why I'm being honest. You deserve more than I can give."

It took months, but Joel eventually found a therapist who specialized in attachment trauma. He wrote Tamara a letter later, thanking her for having the courage to let him go. "I hated you for it at first. Now I understand. You were the first person who trusted me enough to let me struggle."

The Fear of Causing Harm

Guides often worry that ending a relationship will make things worse for the client. That their withdrawal will trigger abandonment wounds, deepen despair, confirm every fear the client carries.

But staying in an unhealthy dynamic doesn't prevent that harm. It just delays it. You become the coping mechanism instead of encouraging the development of one. The client never learns they can survive without you because you never let them try.

Responsible disengagement redirects the client toward broader support. Your absence may feel uncomfortable initially. Discomfort often precedes growth.

Reflections for Your Own Journey

- Have you ever felt responsible for a client's emotional stability? What told you it was happening?
- What part of limiting contact feels most uncomfortable to you?
- Write a calm sentence explaining that communication must remain within sessions.
- How might your practice improve if every client interacted within the same structure?

Professional Distance and the Risk of Over-Familiarization

Longevity in practice is not built on charisma.

It is built on boundaries.

As a spiritual service provider, you will work with people during vulnerable moments — heartbreak, uncertainty, grief, confusion, longing. Clients often feel deeply seen in sessions. They may experience relief, validation, and emotional connection that feels intimate.

This is natural.

But emotional intimacy created within a professional setting is not the same as personal intimacy. Confusing the two is one of the fastest ways to destabilize a hard-earned reputation.

Over-familiarization begins subtly.

Extended messaging outside session structure.
Personal disclosures beyond what is necessary.

Flirtation disguised as warmth.
Private conversations that shift tone from guidance to companionship.

Each step feels small.

The damage, however, is rarely small.

One of the most permanent ways to undermine years of credibility is to enter into sexual or romantic relationships with paying clients. While it may feel consensual, exciting, or harmless in the moment, the power imbalance inherent in a paid guidance relationship complicates everything.

Clients often approach practitioners during periods of heightened emotional vulnerability. Even if both parties believe the relationship is mutual, outside observers — and sometimes the client themselves, once emotions shift — may see it very differently.

What begins as connection can later be reframed as influence.

What feels mutual today, unfortunately, can be described as coercive tomorrow.

And in the age of screenshots, public reviews, and social media amplification, reputational damage spreads faster than clarification.

It is not simply the relationship that creates risk. It is the narrative that can form afterward.

When professional boundaries collapse, the interpretation of past sessions can change. Words once understood as guidance may be reinterpreted as grooming. Emotional validation may be reframed as manipulation. Even if those claims feel unfair, defending against them publicly rarely restores the original trust.

Reputation is built slowly.

It can be weakened quickly.

The Power Imbalance You Cannot Remove

Even if you view yourself as equal to your clients, the structure of the relationship is not neutral.

They pay you.
They seek your insight.
They assign meaning to your words.

That dynamic creates influence — whether you intend it or not.

Influence is not abuse.
But it is responsibility.

When a practitioner crosses into sexual or romantic territory with a client, that influence becomes part of the equation. The relationship is no longer simply personal. It is layered with prior authority, emotional exposure, and financial exchange.

In many professions — therapy, coaching, law, counseling, spiritual direction — such relationships are explicitly prohibited for this reason. The concern is not romance itself. The concern is compromised judgment and the erosion of trust in the profession as a whole.

Even one publicized incident can affect not only your name, but the credibility of others in your field.

The Illusion of "It's Different With Us"

Nearly every professional boundary violation begins with the same internal justification:

"This situation is different."

Perhaps the chemistry feels undeniable.
Perhaps the client insists it is mutual.
Perhaps time has passed since the first session.

But the original dynamic cannot be erased. It becomes part of the story permanently.

Even if the relationship remains positive, the public optics are rarely kind. And if it ends poorly, the fallout can extend far beyond private disagreement.

As the saying goes, emotions shift faster than reputations repair.

The Cost of Scandal in a Trust-Based Field

Spiritual practice depends on perceived integrity.

Your clients are not simply buying time; they are buying trust. They are entrusting you with their fears, their hopes, their most sensitive questions.

When that trust appears compromised, the public reaction is swift.

Reviews change tone.
Colleagues distance themselves.

Referrals decline.
Whispers travel quietly through online communities.

Even if no legal action occurs, reputational damage in a trust-based profession can be profound and long-lasting.

A single allegation can outweigh years of steady work.

Protecting Yourself Through Structure

The safest course is simple and firm:

Do not pursue or accept romantic or sexual involvement with paying clients.

If genuine interest develops, the professional relationship must end completely, and as in many professional fields, sufficient time should pass before any personal relationship is considered. Even then, careful thought is required.

Clear boundaries protect both parties.

They prevent confusion.
They prevent reinterpretation.
They prevent dependency from turning into attachment.

And most importantly, they preserve your ability to continue your work without suspicion.

Longevity Requires Restraint

The practitioner who lasts twenty years is not the one who follows every impulse.

It is the one who understands that momentary gratification can cost long-term credibility.
Professional distance is not coldness.
It is stewardship.

You are not denying connection; you are protecting the integrity of your role. You have wisdom, experience and power that the world needs.

Think beyond the present moment.
Think beyond the excitement of being admired.
Think beyond the assumption that everything will remain amicable.

Ask yourself:

Is this decision aligned with the reputation I am building?

Because while admiration may feel powerful, stability is more powerful still.

And stability is what allows your practice to endure.

Chapter 15:

The Unsexy Essentials — Protecting Yourself, Your Practice, and Your Future

This chapter is different from everything we've covered so far.

We've talked about boundaries with clients, the weight of being trusted, the slow creep of dependence. We've explored the emotional and relational dimensions of this work—the parts that feel meaningful, connected, human.

Now we need to talk about the parts that don't feel any of those things.

The parts that feel bureaucratic. Administrative. Downright unspiritual. The parts that make many practitioners' eyes glaze over, that get pushed to the bottom of to-do lists, that feel like they belong to a different world entirely.

Here's what I've learned after years of watching gifted practitioners struggle: avoiding the unsexy stuff doesn't make it go away. It just means it will ambush you later, usually at the worst possible moment.

A single legal or financial mistake can undo years of careful work. A pricing confusion can lead to burnout that no amount of self-care can fix. A marketing approach that feels "salesy" can keep you invisible and underearning indefinitely.

This chapter is about preventing all of that. Not through fear, but through preparation. Not because you're greedy or paranoid, but because you're professional enough to protect what you've built.

Part One: Marketing Without Feeling Icky

Let's start with the word that makes most spiritual practitioners cringe: marketing.

It conjures images of used car salesmen and pushy influencers and people who care more about commissions than clients. It feels like the opposite of everything you stand for—authenticity, presence, genuine connection.

I understand that reaction. I felt it too, for years.

But here's what I've come to understand: marketing is just telling people you exist so they can decide if you're for them.

That's it. Nothing more. You're not convincing, manipulating, or selling. You're simply making yourself visible to people who might need what you offer. And if you genuinely believe your work helps people, then staying invisible isn't humble—it's withholding.

Finding Your Voice Without Losing Yourself

The key to marketing that doesn't feel gross is simple: don't say anything you wouldn't say to a client sitting across from you.

If you wouldn't tell a real person in a real session that you're "the #1 transformational guide for cosmic alignment," don't put it on your website. If you wouldn't promise someone certainty about their future, don't promise it in your social media posts. Let your public voice be an accurate preview of your private presence.

The practitioners who struggle most with marketing are usually the ones trying to sound like someone else. They adopt a tone they think will attract clients, and it feels hollow because it is hollow. Clients sense that. They may not name it, but they feel the gap between the performance and the person.

Your marketing should sound like you. Calm, clear, honest. The same voice you use in sessions. The same presence you bring to your work. When your public face matches your private one, nothing feels fake—and nothing feels icky.

What to Share, What to Keep

A good rule of thumb: share enough that people understand what you offer, but not so much that they feel they've already received it.

Post about themes you work with. Talk about patterns you see. Offer perspectives that help people think differently. But don't give away the depth of a full session in a social media post.

Leave room for the real work, the one that happens in the container you've built.

People should walk away from your content thinking, "I want more of that." Not, "I already got everything I needed."

The Fear of Being Seen

Behind most marketing resistance lies a quieter fear: what if I put myself out there and no one cares? What if I'm visible and still invisible? What if I try and fail?

This fear is real, and it deserves compassion. But it also deserves perspective. Every practitioner you admire was invisible once. Every guide with a full calendar started with empty ones. Visibility is a process, not an event. You build it gradually, post by post, conversation by conversation, until one day you realize people are finding you without you having to find them first.

Start small. Post something authentic. Share one insight. Write one email. See how it feels. Then do it again. The fear rarely disappears entirely, but it does shrink with practice.

The One Thing That Matters More Than Followers

Here's a truth the algorithms won't tell you: followers don't pay your bills. The people who actually book sessions do.

A thousand followers who never become clients are just a number. Fifty engaged email subscribers who trust you and show up when you offer something—those are a practice. Don't get seduced by metrics that don't matter. Focus on connection, not count.

Building an email list is the single most important marketing move you can make. Social media platforms change their algorithms constantly. They can take your reach away overnight. Your email list is yours. No algorithm touches it. No platform owns it. It's a direct line to people who have already said, "Yes, I want to hear from you."

Start your list now, even if it's just five people. Send them something useful regularly. Over time, that list becomes the foundation of everything you build.

The Testimonial That Doesn't Feel Awkward

Asking for testimonials feels terrible to most guides. It feels like begging, like fishing for compliments, like putting clients on the spot.

But here's a reframe: you're not asking for a favor. You're offering clients a chance to reflect on their experience and honor what shifted for them. Many people want to express gratitude but don't know how. A simple request gives them permission.

Try this: after a session, when a client expresses appreciation, say, "I'm so glad that landed for you. Would you be willing to put a few sentences about your experience in writing? It helps others understand what I offer, and it also helps me remember what's working."

Keep it simple. Don't pressure. If they say no, thank them anyway and move on. The ones who say yes will give you words far more powerful than anything you could write yourself.

Part Two: The Legal and Financial Foundation No One Talks About

Now for the part that makes everyone uncomfortable. Let's just name that up front: this section is not exciting. It's not mystical. It's not going to make your heart sing.

But it might save your practice.

Why Structure Matters More Than You Think

When you're a sole proprietor—which is what most guides are by default—there is no separation between you and your business. Legally and financially, you are your practice. If something goes wrong, if someone sues you, if you have a financial problem—it's not just your business at risk. It's you. Your personal savings. Your home. Your family. Your future.

This isn't fear-mongering. It's reality. And it's also easily addressed.

Forming a simple LLC (Limited Liability Company) creates a legal separation between you and your work. It says, "If something happens with the business, it stays with the business." Your personal assets remain protected. You can sleep easier.

The cost is minimal. The paperwork is manageable. And the peace of mind is incalculable. Talk to a local small business attorney or use an online service. Just do it. Don't let another year pass without this protection in place.

The Bank Account That Changes Everything

Once you have an LLC, open a separate bank account for your business. Run all your income and expenses through it. Pay yourself from it. Never mix personal and business funds.

This single habit will save you countless hours at tax time. It will make your finances visible and manageable. It will prevent the dreaded "where did all the money go" confusion that plagues so many practitioners.

If you're not ready for an LLC yet, at minimum open a separate personal account just for business. Keep them separate. Your future self will thank you.

Disclaimers: Not Just Legal CYA

Many practitioners resist disclaimers because they feel defensive or fear-based. But a good disclaimer isn't about protecting yourself from clients—it's about making sure clients understand what you actually offer.

A simple statement on your website and intake forms can prevent endless misunderstandings:

"The guidance I provide is for informational and educational purposes only. It is not a substitute for professional medical, mental health, financial, or legal advice. You are solely responsible for your own decisions and outcomes."

That's it. Clear, honest, protective. It doesn't say you're useless. It says you're not something you're not. Clients deserve to know the difference.

Taxes: The Topic Everyone Avoids

Here's the truth about taxes and spiritual work: the IRS doesn't care if your income came from intuitive guidance or dog walking. It's all income. It's all taxable. And ignoring that fact doesn't make it less true.

If you're earning money from your practice, you need to:

- Track every dollar that comes in
- Track every dollar you spend on your business (sessions, software, education, website costs, etc.)
- Set aside roughly 25-30% of each payment for taxes (more if you're in a high-tax state)
- Pay estimated quarterly taxes if you owe more than $1,000 per year

This sounds overwhelming, but it becomes simple with systems. Use accounting software. Hire a bookkeeper for a few hours each month. Find an accountant who works with small business owners. The money you spend on professional help will come back many times over in avoided stress and penalties.

Insurance: Hopefully You'll Never Need It

Professional liability insurance (sometimes called "errors and omissions" insurance) is exactly what it sounds like: coverage if a client claims you caused them harm.

You hope you'll never need it. You probably never will. But the one time something goes sideways—a misunderstanding, a distressed client, a claim that has no merit but still requires response—you will be grateful beyond words that you have it.

Policies for spiritual practitioners are surprisingly affordable. Look for insurers who understand this work. Read the fine print. Make sure you're covered for the specific services you offer. Then file the policy away and forget about it, knowing it's there if you need it.

Part Three: Pricing, Packaging, and Actually Getting Paid

We talked earlier about money mindset. Now let's talk about money mechanics.

How to Set Your Rates (Without Guessing)

There's a common myth that pricing is mystical—that you should just charge "what feels right" and trust the universe to provide. I understand the impulse. But in my experience, the universe works better with clear information.

Here's a practical way to set your rates:

1. Calculate your baseline. How much money do you need to live on per month? Be honest. Include rent, food, savings, fun. This is your floor.
2. Calculate your capacity. How many sessions can you sustainably offer per week? Not maximum—sustainable.

The number you could maintain for years without burning out.

3. Do the math. Divide your monthly need by your weekly sessions (times four weeks). That's your minimum viable rate. If you charge less than this, you'll either burn out from overwork or resent your clients for underpaying.
4. Add value. Now add 20-30% to that number. This accounts for your experience, your skill, your overhead, and the simple fact that you're worth more than minimum viable.
5. Test it. Charge that rate for three months. See how it feels. See who books. Adjust as needed.

This isn't greedy. It's sustainable. And sustainability is the most caring thing you can offer, because it means you'll still be here next year.

The Raise Conversation

At some point, you'll need to raise your rates. This is terrifying for almost everyone. But it's also necessary. Your skills grow. Your experience deepens. Your costs increase. Your rates should reflect that.

When you raise rates:

- Give existing clients plenty of notice (30-60 days)
- Explain simply: "As my practice evolves, I'm adjusting my rates to reflect the depth of work I now offer."
- Don't apologize
- Offer a grace period for current clients to book at the old rate
- Hold steady when someone pushes back

Some clients will leave when you raise rates. This is normal and okay. They weren't your long-term people. The ones who stay will respect you more, not less, for valuing your own work.

Packages, Subscriptions, and Single Sessions

Different clients need different ways to engage. Offering options can serve more people without creating more chaos.

- Single sessions work well for new clients, occasional check-ins, and focused questions.
- Packages (three or six sessions prepaid) encourage deeper work and provide income stability for you.
- Subscriptions (monthly recurring payments for ongoing support) work for clients who want regular check-ins and predictable access.
- Intensives (longer, deeper sessions) serve clients with specific issues that need concentrated attention.

Each option has pros and cons. Test different models and see what resonates. The key is clarity: whatever you offer, make the terms visible and consistent.

Sliding Scales and Pro Bono Work

Many practitioners want to make their work accessible to those with less money. This is beautiful. It's also a recipe for resentment if not structured carefully.

If you offer sliding scale:

- Define the range clearly (e.g., $50-100)

- Trust clients to self-select into the right bracket
- Limit the number of sliding scale spots (e.g., two per week)
- Never let sliding scale clients fill your entire calendar

If you offer pro bono work:

- Define the terms (e.g., one free session per month for BIPOC clients)
- Make the application process clear
- Treat pro bono clients with the same respect as paying ones because there are still legal obligations when you tell someone you will provide a service on a voluntary basis
- Never let guilt drive your giving

Generosity is wonderful. Generosity without boundaries is self-destruction.

Late Payments, No-Shows, and Cancellations

Every practitioner eventually faces the client who doesn't pay, doesn't show, or cancels at the last minute. Having clear policies beforehand prevents these moments from becoming personal.

Your policy should include:

- When payment is due (before the session, at booking)
- How far in advance cancellations are accepted (24-48 hours)
- What happens after that window (full session fee charged)
- What constitutes an emergency exception (use sparingly)
- How repeated no-shows are handled

Communicate this policy everywhere—website, intake forms, booking confirmations. When someone challenges it, you're not saying no personally. You're just following the policy that applies to everyone.

Part Four: Systems That Set You Free

The word "systems" sounds rigid. But good systems don't restrict you—they free you. They handle the mundane so your mind can handle the meaningful.

Scheduling That Doesn't Drain You

Manual scheduling is exhausting. Back-and-forth emails about availability. Clients who forget time zones. Double-bookings and confusion. All of it drains energy you could be using for actual work.

Scheduling software solves this. Options like Calendly, Acuity, or Vagaro integrate with your calendar, show your real-time availability, and let clients book themselves. They send reminders, handle rescheduling, and collect intake information automatically.

The investment is minimal. The return in mental space is enormous.

Payment Processing Made Simple

Similarly, let software handle payments. Stripe, Square, and PayPal all integrate with scheduling platforms. Clients pay at booking. You don't chase invoices. Money appears in your account automatically.

If you're nervous about fees, remember: the time you save is worth more than the percentage you pay. And clients appreciate the ease of seamless payment.

Intake Forms That Actually Help

A good intake form does more than collect contact information. It prepares clients for the session and gives you useful context beforehand.

Ask for:

- Name, contact, emergency contact (if relevant)
- What brings them now
- What they hope to gain
- Previous experience with this kind of work
- Any relevant medical or mental health context
- Agreement to your policies and disclaimer

Review this form before each session. It takes five minutes and grounds you in their world before you even speak.

Notes That Protect Everyone

You don't need detailed transcripts, but you do need records. Simple notes after each session:

- Date and duration
- General themes discussed
- Any commitments or takeaways
- Observations about their state

These notes aren't for therapy. They're for continuity—so if a client returns in six months, you remember where you left off. They're also protection, providing documentation if questions arise later.

Keep notes securely. Password-protected files, encrypted if possible. Treat client information with the same care you'd want for your own.

Office Hours and Availability

One of the simplest sanity-preserving systems is defined availability. You're not on call 24/7. You have hours when you're available for sessions, and hours when you're not.

Communicate these clearly. Set expectations about response times for messages (24-48 hours is reasonable). Use auto-responders when you're out of office. Let technology hold the boundary so you don't have to.

Clients adapt quickly to clear rhythms. They stop expecting immediate responses when they've never received them. You stop feeling guilty for not responding because the expectation was never created.

Part Five: The Hard Conversations You'll Eventually Need

No matter how well you build your practice, difficult situations will arise. Being prepared for them is the difference between crisis and merely uncomfortable.

When a Client Doesn't Pay

It happens. Someone books, receives their session, and then the payment doesn't go through. Or disputes the charge. Or simply never pays.

First, check in. Sometimes it's a genuine error. Reach out calmly: "I noticed the payment didn't process. Can you help me understand what happened?"

If they resist or refuse, follow your policy. If you have none, you're negotiating emotionally. If you have one, you're just implementing it: "As outlined in our agreement, payment is due at time of service. I'll need to pause future bookings until this is resolved."

Most people pay when reminded. Some won't. For the ones who won't, consider whether pursuing it is worth your energy. Sometimes the cost of collection exceeds the amount owed. Let it go, learn the lesson, and tighten your prepayment requirements.

When a Client Crosses a Line

Boundary violations come in many forms: romantic advances, aggressive messages, refusal to respect time limits, personal questions that feel invasive.

Your response should be immediate and calm. "I'm noticing this conversation moving in a direction that doesn't feel appropriate for our work together. Let's return to the focus of the session."

If it continues, be clearer: "I need to maintain a professional container for our work. If you're unable to respect that, we may need to pause or end our time together."

You are allowed to end a session early. You are allowed to decline future sessions. You are allowed to protect yourself. No client is worth your safety or peace.

When You Need to Fire a Client

Sometimes the relationship just isn't working. The client isn't benefiting. You're dreading sessions. The dynamic has become unhealthy.

Firing a client is uncomfortable, but it's also responsible. You're not helping them by continuing a dynamic that isn't working.

A simple script: "I've been reflecting on our work together, and I don't feel I'm the right person to support you at this time. I want you to get the help you deserve, and I think that might come better from someone else. I'm happy to provide referrals if that would be helpful."

No blame. No long explanations. Just a clean ending that preserves dignity for both of you. When you need to end a professional relationship put it into writing in order to protect yourself. If you need to access the information to protect yourself at a later time you will have it as evidence of when and why you terminated the professional relationship.

When You Need Help

The most important thing to know: you don't have to figure this out alone.

Accountants, lawyers, bookkeepers, coaches, mentors—these people exist because every profession has parts that require specialized knowledge. Paying for their help isn't failure. It's wisdom.

Find an accountant who works with small business owners. Consult a lawyer for your LLC and contracts. Hire a bookkeeper for a few hours each month. Join a mastermind or peer supervision group where you can ask questions and learn from others further along.

The money you spend on professional help will come back many times over in avoided mistakes, reduced stress, and freed-up energy for the work you actually love.

Part Six: Planning for Your Absence

This is the topic no one wants to think about, which is exactly why it needs to be included.

Taking Time Off

You will need breaks. Vacations. Sick days. Mental health days. Times when you simply cannot work.

If you have no plan for these moments, you'll either work through them (and burn out) or cancel last minute (and disappoint clients). Neither is sustainable.

Build time off into your calendar from the beginning. Block out vacation weeks in advance. Have a clear cancellation policy that covers illness. Communicate your availability windows so clients know when you're present and when you're not.

If you're gone for longer periods, consider:

- A waitlist for when you return
- Referrals to trusted colleagues
- Email auto-responders setting expectations
- Clear communication about when you'll be back

Your clients will survive without you. They might even grow stronger.

If Something Happens to You

This is hard to write and harder to read. But responsible practice includes planning for your own absence.

What happens to your clients if you become unable to work? What happens to your income? Your website? Your email list? Your obligations?

At minimum:

- Tell someone close to you about your practice—where your files are, who your accountant is, what your wishes are
- Have a plan for notifying clients if you're incapacitated

- Consider digital legacy options for your content
- Think about who might step in to help transition clients to other providers

This isn't morbid. It's care. The same care you extend to clients in their lives, extended to them in the event of yours.

Closing a Practice Gracefully

One day, you'll stop doing this work. Maybe you'll retire. Maybe you'll shift to something else. Maybe health or life circumstances will intervene.

Closing a practice is an act of completion. It deserves the same thoughtfulness as everything else you've done.

Give yourself time. Months, ideally. Communicate clearly with clients. Offer referrals. Help them transition. Honor what you've built together.

Then close the door, grateful for what you've done, ready for whatever comes next.

Part Seven: The Company You Keep

Isolation is one of the biggest threats to a long practice. You weren't meant to do this alone.

Finding Your People

Other practitioners understand things that friends and family can't. They know the weight of holding client stories. They know the weirdness of explaining your work at parties. They know the specific exhaustion that comes from deep listening.

Find them. Online or in person. Masterminds, supervision groups, informal gatherings. Spaces where you can talk honestly about the work without having to explain or defend.

Referral Relationships

You can't help everyone. Some clients need things you don't offer—therapy, financial planning, medical care, legal help. Having trusted colleagues to refer to is essential.

Build relationships with:

- Therapists who understand spiritual work
- Financial advisors who work with creatives
- Bodyworkers, acupuncturists, other holistic providers
- Career coaches, relationship counselors, grief specialists

When you refer someone, you're not failing them. You're giving them exactly what they need. And they'll remember that you cared enough to connect them properly.

Handling Competition Jealousy

Another practitioner gets more clients than you. Has a bigger following. Seems to be thriving while you're struggling. Jealousy rises.

This is human. Don't shame yourself for it. But don't let it rule you either.

Remember: their success doesn't limit yours. There are more than enough people needing help. Someone else's full calendar doesn't empty yours. Their visibility doesn't make you invisible.

If jealousy keeps arising, get curious. What are they doing that you're not? What fears is their success triggering? What might you learn from them instead of resenting them?

Giving Back

At some point, you'll have experience worth sharing. Mentoring newer practitioners. Offering workshops. Writing. Teaching.

This isn't required, but it is meaningful. Passing on what you've learned completes a cycle. It reminds you how far you've come. It connects you to the next generation of guides.

When you're ready, find ways to give back. Not from obligation, but from abundance.

Part Eight: Continuing Education

You'll never know everything. The best practitioners are the ones still learning.

Staying Fresh

The work can become rote if you're not careful. Same patterns, same issues, same responses. Clients still benefit, but you stop growing.

Keep learning. Read books outside your field. Take courses. Attend workshops. Explore modalities you don't offer. Let yourself be a beginner sometimes.

Your clients will benefit from your continued growth. A stale guide helps less than one still curious.

Supervision and Consultation

Even experienced practitioners benefit from consultation. A fresh set of eyes on a stuck case. A sounding board for an ethical question. A space to process the weight you carry.

Find a supervisor or consultant. Pay them for their time. Treat it as essential professional development, not optional extras.

Knowing Your Limits

The more you learn, the more you'll recognize what you don't know. This is progress, not failure.

When a client's needs exceed your expertise, refer out. When a situation feels beyond you, say so. When you're uncertain, admit it.

Clients trust guides who know their limits. Pretending you know everything is the fastest way to lose credibility.

Reflections for Your Own Journey

- What part of marketing feels most uncomfortable? What fear might be underneath it?

- Do you have legal and financial separation between you and your practice? If not, what's one step you could take this month?
- How did you set your current rates? Do they reflect your actual needs and capacity?
- What systems could you put in place this week to reduce mental load?
- Who's in your professional community? If no one, where might you start looking?
- What happens to your clients if you're unexpectedly unavailable? Do you have a plan?
- What's one area where you'd like to keep learning? What's stopping you?

This chapter won't make your heart sing. It won't deepen your intuition or sharpen your insights. But it might save your practice. And a saved practice can keep helping people for years to come.

That's the point. Not just doing good work, but doing it in a way that lasts. Protecting what you've built so it can keep serving. Building systems that free you to do what only you can do.

The unsexy essentials aren't the enemy of your calling. They're the foundation that lets your calling stand.

Chapter 16:

The Guides Who Last

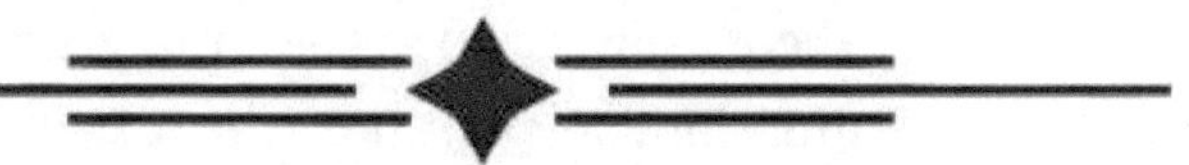

At the beginning, everything feels urgent.

Building the practice. Finding clients. Getting better at your work. Handling each new challenge as it arises. Energy is high, and you throw yourself into everything because it all matters, it's all important, it's all part of becoming who you're meant to be.

Then time passes.

You have sessions that drain instead of fill. You encounter clients who challenge instead of grow. You see patterns repeat across different people, different stories, different pain. The work that once felt fresh starts to feel familiar. The energy that once seemed endless starts to flicker.

This is where many practices quietly end. Not through failure, but through depletion. The guide didn't lose their gift. They just ran out of gas.

But some guides last. Twenty years, thirty years, more. They're still present, still steady, still showing up with clarity and care. They're not necessarily the most famous or dramatic guides. They're the most sustainable.

What They Do Differently

Long-term guides share a quiet internal shift: they stop trying to resolve everything.

They accept that their role is to assist thinking, not finalize outcomes. Once this lands, pressure decreases dramatically. Success is no longer measured by whether events occur. It's measured by whether clients leave clearer than they arrived.

Clarity is repeatable. Outcomes aren't.

The Guide Who Learned to Release

I met a guide named Harold when he'd been practicing for over forty years. He was in his seventies, still seeing clients, still doing the work with the same presence he'd had decades earlier. I asked him how he'd sustained it for so long.

"When I was young," he said, "I carried every client home with me. I'd lie awake worrying about them, wondering if they were okay, feeling responsible for their happiness. It nearly destroyed me."

He paused, then continued. "One day, an older guide said something I've never forgotten. She said, 'You're not the author of their story. You're just a helpful footnote.' Something in me relaxed. I stopped trying to write their lives and started just showing up for the pages they were living."

Harold still cared deeply. He was still present, still attentive, still fully engaged during sessions. But when the session ended, he let it go. He'd done his part. The rest belonged to them.

The Value of Routine

Guides who last rarely operate spontaneously. They maintain:

- Regular session schedules
- Consistent preparation habits
- Defined ending rituals
- Clear separation between work and rest

Routine signals the mind when to engage and when to disengage. Without it, emotional residue accumulates. With it, attention renews.

Continual Simplification

Early guides often expand—more services, more availability, more communication channels. Long-term guides refine.

They narrow focus to what works consistently. They remove offerings that create confusion or disproportionate effort. They say no more than they say yes.

Simplicity supports endurance. A clear practice is easier to maintain than a constantly changing one.

The Role of Rest

Your personal life affects your professional clarity. Guides who last maintain boundaries around rest, relationships, private time.

They don't treat availability as proof of dedication. They treat steadiness as proof of care.

A rested guide perceives better than an exhausted one. Longevity requires respecting your own capacity as part of ethical practice.

The Client Who Came Back to Thank Me

Years ago, I worked with a woman named Nora who was going through a terrible divorce. She was angry, hurt, lost—all the things you'd expect. We met regularly for about a year, and then she moved away and I lost touch.

Last month, she found me again. She wasn't a client anymore. She just wanted to say thank you.

"I think about our sessions sometimes," she told me. "Not for the predictions or the advice. For the way you just sat with me. You didn't try to fix it or make it better. You just... stayed. That taught me something I've carried ever since."

I didn't remember anything remarkable about our work together. I remembered Nora, vaguely, but not the details. And yet, something I'd done—some ordinary, unremarkable act of presence—had stayed with her for years.

That's the legacy of consistency. Not dramatic transformation, but reliable presence during uncertainty. Not fixing, but staying. Not resolving, but holding space for resolution to emerge on its own.

What Endures

A practice survives decades when:

- Boundaries stay clear
- Language stays measured
- Structure stays consistent
- Self-care stays intentional

None of this depends on trends or visibility. It depends on decisions made daily. Small choices, repeated endlessly, that add up to something solid enough to last.

Longevity isn't achieved through extraordinary ability. It's achieved through sustainable behavior, repeated quietly, over time.

Reflections for Your Own Journey

- What part of your current practice feels hardest to sustain long-term?
- Which responsibility do you carry that doesn't actually belong to your role?
- What simple routine could help you mentally end sessions each day?
- If your practice still existed twenty years from now, what would it look like?

A Final Thought

We've covered a lot of ground together.

The weight of being seen. The slow creep of dependence. The quiet difference between being liked and being trusted. The boundaries that protect everyone. The money conversations nobody wants to have. The clients who need more than you can give. The recognition that comes from consistency, not drama.

None of this was meant to change what you offer. It was meant to stabilize how you offer it.

Your gift brought people to you. Your structure will allow you to remain for them. Not as someone who's always certain, always available, always right. But as someone who's steady. Someone who can be relied upon, session after session, year after year, to show up with the same clarity, the same presence, the same care.

That steadiness is the foundation of real trust. Not being impressive. Not being dramatic. Not being needed. Just being there, reliably, in the ways you've promised.

The people who come to you are looking for solid ground. Be solid enough to hold them—and solid enough to let them go when they're ready to stand on their own.

That's the work. That's always been the work. And now you have the tools to do it, cleanly and clearly, for as long as you choose.

Go well.

www.ingramcontent.com/pod-product-compliance
Lightning Source LLC
LaVergne TN
LVHW090530110826
845146LV00003B/1042

* 9 7 9 8 9 9 5 1 6 1 7 1 4 *